STUDIES IN HISTORY, ECONOMICS AND
PUBLIC LAW

Edited by the

FACULTY OF POLITICAL SCIENCE
OF COLUMBIA UNIVERSITY

———

Number 568

THE PURITAN FRONTIER
TOWN-PLANTING IN NEW ENGLAND
COLONIAL DEVELOPMENT 1630-1660

BY

WILLIAM HALLER, Jr.

THE PURITAN FRONTIER
TOWN-PLANTING IN NEW ENGLAND
COLONIAL DEVELOPMENT 1630-1660

BY

WILLIAM HALLER, Jr

AMS PRESS
NEW YORK

COLUMBIA UNIVERSITY
STUDIES IN THE
SOCIAL SCIENCES

568

The Series was formerly known as
Studies in History, Economics and Public Law.

Reprinted with the permission of Columbia University Press
From the edition of 1951, New York
First AMS EDITION published 1968
Manufactured in the United States of America

Library of Congress Catalogue Card Number: 78-76657

AMS PRESS, INC.
NEW YORK, N. Y. 10003

To My Father

FOREWORD

THE work which follows is the result of an attempt to discover some of the relationships between the development of human ideas and that of economic institutions in a fairly narrow geographical and historical setting. The communities studied were small and new, the people were coping with new problems in an unfamiliar environment and so the period and region seemed one in which substantial and significant developments could be found in a fairly small compass. The interpreter of these developments could use a very extensive body of historical research and writing as a background and focus attention on those aspects which seem relevant to the problems in hand.

Whoever knows his work will understand that my father has contributed much to my task. I must record my gratitude to him, not only for scholarly insight, but for financial support and paternal patience and encouragement. Professor Carter Goodrich of Columbia University, as my principal adviser in this project, has given his time and wisdom most generously, and Professor Joseph Dorfman has offered similar valuable help.

The libraries of Amherst College, Columbia University and the University of Massachusetts, the American Antiquarian Association of Worcester, Massachusetts, the Forbes Library of Northampton, Massachusetts and the New York Public library have opened their resources to me. Ruth Haller's assistance has been of incalculable value.

TABLE OF CONTENTS

PART I

The Puritan Design for Frontier Development

PART II

Town-planting as a Technique of Frontier Development

9

PART I

THE PURITAN DESIGN FOR FRONTIER DEVELOPMENT

CHAPTER I

INTRODUCTION

NEW ENGLAND in 1620 was a region in which Europeans had explored but had not yet built permanent settlements. Forty years later, about a hundred English communities lined the coast from Maine to Long Island Sound and the rivers and inland trails of the region. Households, enterprises and local governments were attaining an orderly adaptation of the resources of the environment to the ends which the colonists believed important. The region and the period have been the subject of extensive historical study. They provide an opportunity to study, in a rapidly changing and growing community, the relation between the ideas and habits by which men govern their economic activities, and the extent and character of available natural resources. The Puritan colonists arrived in New England with a well-developed theory of what civilized society was, how it grew and how its future growth should be planned. They brought with them laws, political institutions and habits of land ownership and commercial behaviour in which were reflected Puritan idealism, English tradition and adaptation to the exigencies of colonial life. They planted towns which were carefully devised organizations to promote the development of ecclesiastical, political and economic activities. As they lived in New England, they learned, and as they learned, both theories and institutions were bent but not broken in contact with the facts of the physical environment.

Plymouth was the first English settlement in the region which grew into a permanent settled community. Its population before 1629 was minute compared with that of the New England colonies in the following decade. Like the later settlements it included an articulate and influential group actuated by religious idealism and dissatisfaction with the current state of the Church of England. The Massachusetts Bay Company passed in 1629 into the control of a group similarly motivated, which from 1630 to 1640 induced thousands of emigrating Englishmen to land in their jurisdiction. Connecticut was planted by some of these who found reason to emigrate again, this time from Massachusetts, Rhode Island by colonists alienated by a clash of opinion from the leaders of the older colony, and the short-lived New Haven colony by new arrivals who found themselves better pleased with the unclaimed site they chose than with the remaining lands which the Bay colony could offer.

Plymouth, the Cape Ann and Salem plantations of 1624-1629 and the original Massachusetts Bay towns of 1630 were all settled by people who disembarked in virtually uninhabited wilderness. They improvised shelter, lived on transported provisions and were dependent on the long and uncertain transatlantic supply line. But by 1631 the newly-arriving colonist would frequently be received by a relative, master, servant or friend and would in any event find rudimentary lodgings and a local supply of provisions ready for him to buy or earn. Thereafter the new homes and towns of New England were set down, not in the midst of a howling wilderness, but on an awe-inspiring but receding frontier behind which was the settled safety of permanent civilized communities.

Already in 1630 some of the colonists felt impelled to fare forth to a new plantation at Aggawam in the northern wilderness.[1] In the years that followed, individuals, towns, churches and colonial governments were actively engaged in absorbing the flow of new immigration and fostering and directing the process whereby increased numbers gained access to larger areas. A wave of new town-planting started about 1634 and continued into the early 1640's, and thereafter a year rarely went by without one or more additions to the list of settlements. Traders and professional surveyors pushed further into the wilderness, and households and towns stood ready to accept and occupy grants of land which seemed to promise useful and profitable crops.

1 Mass. Records, I, 76.

The Englishmen who came to New England in the decade of the 1630's were for the most part members of the large and loosely-organized Puritan movement. The decade in which they decided to come was one in which their cause was suffering a series of setbacks in England. Charles I was attempting to rule without Parliament, and his policy seemed to threaten alarming changes in the status of middle-class Englishmen. His appointee, Archbishop Laud, found that Puritan clergymen were not readily adaptable to his concept of ecclesiastical government and made it more and more difficult for them to continue earning a living either in the established Church or by writing and privately-supported preaching.

A substantial number of ministers found themselves deprived of livings in the Church, or more or less harassed in their pulpits by an unsympathetic hierarchy. An even greater number of laymen found it increasingly difficult to get the kind of preaching, teaching and guidance they wanted, either from the Church or through private chaplains and lecturers. Many of the heads of households who came to New England thought the opportunity to avoid these difficulties one of the attractive inducements to undertake the move. A fair number of the ministers who came arrived in the company of considerable groups of neighbors and former parishioners. Others were called to the colonies by admirers who preceded them, and still others, once settled in a new plantation, served as an inducement to emigration among their following in the mother country.

Estimates of numbers of people in, or numbers of immigrants into the colonies are commonly based on enumerations for tax or militia purposes, on contemporary counts of the number of ships and passengers, and on the observations of contemporary travelers and observers. These are obviously imperfect methods of estimation. Such as they are, they justify a guess that the population of the five New England colonies had risen by 1640 to nearly 20,000, mostly by immigration since 1630, and that it grew by some thousands between 1640 and 1660. In the 1620's there were no more than a few hundred settlers. The 1630's saw the most rapid percentage increase, and probably a rate of immigration higher than that of the decades next following. From about 1642 to 1660 there were probably fewer English newcomers, but natural increase contributed substantially to growth during that period.[2]

The new policy and personnel of the Massachusetts Bay Company in 1629 was the forerunner of a strong movement of new colonists. In that year John Endicott was sent as Governor of the settlers already at Salem, and a small party came with him. In the summer of 1630 some hundreds of colonists disembarked in and around Boston harbor, and in the following years still more followed them. Until about 1634 practically all the newcomers settled in the eight original towns of the colony. By that time people in these towns were becoming more and more aware of the relative density of population there

2 Franklin Bowditch Dexter, "Estimates of Population in the American Colonies." *Report of the Council of the American Antiquarian Society,* Worcester, 1887.

U. S. Department of Commerce and Labor, Bureau of the Census, S. N. D. North, Director, *A Century of Population Growth,* Washington, D. C., 1909.

Evarts B. Greene and Virginia Harrington, *American Population before the Federal Census of 1790,* New York, 1932.

The first two present estimates based on their evaluation of historical evidence which they review, the Census Bureau's report depending partly on Dexter's work. Greene and Harrington present a collection of contemporaneous estimates.

The Census Bureau tabulates the following figures, which are apparently decennial interpolations of their estimates:

	1620	1630	1640	1650	1660
Maine		400	700	1000	a
New Hampshire		500	800	1400	2300
Massachusetts	99	1300	14,000	18,000	25,000 a
Rhode Island			300	800	1500
Connecticut			2000	6,000	8,000
Total New England population	99	2200	17,800	27,200	36,800

a Maine included in Massachusetts in 1660.

These figures are for modern state areas as nearly as possible, which correspond nearly but not precisely to the colonies at that time. They include Plymouth colony with Massachusetts and New Haven with Connecticut.

Greene and Harrington quote figures both above and below these in nearby years.

and the advantages to be gained by spreading out over a larger area. From 1634 to 1640 a substantial share of the population increase was passed on to new towns, and the habit of frontier town-planting came into being.

By 1640 the novelty of town planting was wearing off. Thereafter it was less likely to take place in an atmosphere of tense group solidarity, of stern partings, of the high emotion with which the Puritans gathered a church and signed a covenant. It was carried on under less pressure, too, as the wave of migration subsided. In 1640 Parliament met again and the Puritans among its members and supporters found it an increasingly effective pulpit and debating ground, and finally a tool and weapon of reformation even more valuable and hopeful than the overseas proving ground where so many had gone to test their ideas. The years from 1640 to 1642 saw a lessening of immigration and also a lowering of intellectual and emotional pressure as more of the ministers and of the strongly articulate Puritans remained in England.

The basic unit of organized society in New England was the plantation. As grantee or claimant of a tract of land, it managed the common property of the households of which it was composed. It ordinarily supported a town government exercising considerable power and responsibility. Its organization grew beside and paralleled that of the congregational church without which it would find survival difficult and legal recognition often impossible.

Plantations varied greatly in the number of people and families constituting them, but within limits. There are very few cases where single households planted by themselves, and some evidence that both official and public opinion frowned on isolated homesteads. In some plantations seven householders were regarded as the least number that could form a church or subscribe to a plantation covenant. Massachusetts Bay required the grantees of some town sites to settle ten, twenty or a " sufficient number " of families before the grant became effective. Roger Williams, who was more at home among the Indians than the average colonist and less a respecter of the established colonies' law and traditions, soon gathered other men and households around his home at Providence. The isolated homesteads and farms of the period before 1660 were exceptional and non-conforming occurrences, and very few in number.

At the upper limit of size,[3] plantations or towns which became too populous for their circumstances had a strong tendency either to split in two or to produce offshoot plantations as an outlet for population growth. As we shall see, this tendency to grow and split became one of the characteristic steps in the process of frontier development.

A plantation required three institutional foundation stones. It needed effective possession of a tract of land, a political structure and a gathered church. All of these were on occasion provided by the members of the group without the assistance of outside authority, but for all a centralized colony-wide and intercolonial pattern of control came to be typical. All that was required to gather a congregational Church was any small number of Christians willing to agree to worship together. They might govern their affairs through Ruling Elders, call and ordain one or more ministers and tax themselves and the plantation for church purposes. But after a time, in all the colonies except Rhode Island, existing churches, synods and colonial governments developed tests of orthodoxy to which all congregations and preachers were required to conform. A number of plantations occupied land with no formal title to it, but the colonial governments eventually laid claim to all the available land and required new towns to obtain grants from them. Some towns established local government by a covenant in which the householders agreed to render obedience to authority which their leaders exercised in the name of the Crown or of

3 A numerical estimate of this limit would be only an approximation, and would not be the same for different towns and times. It would perhaps be more accurate to speak of a critical zone of population values in which pressure was likely to be felt. These tendencies appeared sometimes in towns of about 200 households, but sometimes in larger or smaller ones.

Divine Ordinance, or simply assumed in response to the exigencies of the situation. But individual towns became subdivisions of colonies by annexation or federation, and new ones received a grant of municipal authority from colonial governments.

Plantations and towns were essentially aggregations of households for purposes of social cooperation. The household was governed and represented in the community by its head. It usually included also the householder's wife and children and frequently other kinsfolk, apprentices and servants. The latter were usually indentured for a term of years, and the law and political authority regarded them as subject to family authority. Single men, though commonly found, were something of a social anomaly. They might, if they had the resources, become householders themselves. Failing that, they were likely to be pressed or required to submit to family government.

A householder would ordinarily be admitted as inhabitant of a town only by the consent of existing inhabitants. As such, he was entitled to a voice and a vote in town affairs, liable for payment of local and colony rates in proportion to some measure of the value of his estate and, if he was an early arrival or a purchaser of someone's common right, entitled to share in the use and division of the common lands of the town. Unless he was an admitted inhabitant, a man would usually not have the right to build a dwelling house, even on purchased land. The town might require him to provide a bond and sureties that he would not become its poor-relief liability and was entitled, if he failed to do so, to order him out of town after a specified period.

The householder who was an admitted inhabitant was, so to speak, a member of the lowest order of citizenship. His rights and responsibilities arose from his relationship with the local unit of government and land-ownership, whereas those of subordinate members of households were governed by husband, father, guardian or master. He ordinarily owned land and a house, had tax liabilities and a limited share in the processes of local government.

For adult men, admission as an inhabitant was fairly easy to attain, though not automatic. Many if not most indentured servants became land-owners and family heads within a few years after the end of their terms, in their old or a new town. Sons of householders inherited or received gifts of parental land, purchased land or common rights or moved to new towns. Towns tried to see to it that their members were men with the tools, manpower and habits of industry to be capable of supporting their households and bearing their share of public charges.

A large number, though by no means all the families that came to New England included one or more servants, who might be men, women or teen-age children.[4] Some colonists arranged with friends or business correspondents in England to have indentured servants sent to them, others sent servants ahead to the colonies to prepare the way for themselves. Probably some travelers and merchants made a practice of importing man- and woman-power in this form as a commercial venture. At any rate, the buying, selling and trading of indentures was common.

We can find enough cases of men whose term of indenture had expired becoming landowners, householders and heads of families to encourage us to believe that this servile group was not bound in the toils of a rigid caste system. Plymouth colony followed fairly regularly the practice of granting twenty-five acres of unmanured land to those whose terms expired. Towns elsewhere granted houselots to former servants or allowed them to purchase and inhabit.

There were a few men who continued as servants, tenants or family retainers to households usually more than ordinarily well-to-do. Other members of the servile group, usually aged, widowed or orphaned, became destitute and were either boarded or bound to service by the towns in the tradition of

4 Banks, *Planters of the Commonwealth* assembles passenger lists of immigrant ships for 1620-1640. These lists show something of the sort of family group that arrived.

the English poor law. Idle and irresponsible single men might be bound to service, and the children of improvident parents apprenticed or indentured by town governments or courts.

The family and household group was the basis on which the social order of the Puritan plantations was constructed. The legal and customary controls applying to the social status of an individual tended to push him either to attain family headship or to accept subordinate membership. There was sufficient natural wealth, not much disparity in training and natural capacity and no spectacular opportunities for exclusive enjoyment of special advantages by strategically placed individuals, so that the typical adult man in New England was not permanently forced into a servile position. But the household head had to prove his capacity by showing a suitable combination of inherited wealth or worth, industriousness, social morality and business acumen.

As status in the general system of social and economic cooperation was subject to tests of capacity, so membership in the congregational churches was limited to those who demonstrated the effectiveness of their calling as regenerate Christians. To experience a full emotional acceptance of Divine election and sanctification and to confess in open meeting to one's past depravity and present regeneration were prerequisites to acceptance as a communicating church member. The body of the church so constituted chose laymen as Ruling Elders, who administered the income and property of the church and exercised disciplinary authority over the congregation and town. It called and ordained ministers, whose salary was a charge against the whole town. As a group with special political rights and powers and a highly developed organizational discipline and psychological unity, the church was an important instrument of social leadership and control.

Church membership was open to anyone who qualified spiritually and morally. There were no property or status requirements. Men and women, rich and poor, masters and servants,

even one at least of the few Negroes in New England were
church members. So far as formal admission to communion
was concerned, the congregation cut across class lines. But this
was not a pure selective democracy of the elect. For one thing,
in the church meeting wives, sons and servants were under
pretty strong moral pressure to accept the views of their civil
superiors. For another, the disciplinary authority of the officers
of the Church included not only virtual power of excommuni-
cation but also the invocation of political and legal penalties for
ecclesiastical disorder and heresy.

The most powerful figure in a congregational Church was
likely to be the minister. Professionally trained, devoting his
full time to religious affairs and receiving usually a moderate
and comfortable livelihood for his services, he had a moral
standing and strategic position which gave him great power.
Where others spoke their minds in meeting at the risk of being
accused of tumultuous disorder, he had at least one full day a
week to expound and exhort before the whole community.
Typically a university-trained man, he could appeal to Scripture and to a respected body of learning in giving public instruction and private advice. He and his colleagues through
informal cooperation and in regular formal meetings strongly
influenced the attitude of colonial governments and the general
public toward ecclesiastical and political problems.

Colonial citizenship was formally membership in a corporate
or quasi-corporate body of freemen. Tacitly in Massachusetts,
explicitly in Connecticut the franchise was limited to admitted
householding inhabitants of towns. Few were made freemen
who were not members of churches. Probably never more than
a minor fraction of the adult men in the New England colonies
were freemen.

The franchise included the obligation to accept election to
political office. From three to twelve selectmen in each town
usually met several times a year to administer the town's property, manage the common lands and direct the division of land
among the commoners. The constable, annually nominated by

the town and installed in office by the colony or county court,
was not only police officer but collector of town and colony
taxes. Responsibility for roads, schools, weights and measures,
common fields, fences, and pastures was divided among an as-
sortment of specialized local officials. Towns were expected to
send deputies to colonial General Courts, which performed
legislative and judicial duties. Magisrates sat in the General
Court and conducted colony and county court sessions, while
commissioners for small causes were active as local judicial
officers.

At times the burden of these duties was onerous enough so
that penalties were threatened for refusal to serve, or non-freemen appointed to minor local offices. Some towns repeatedly
failed to send their deputies to General Court sessions. A substantial number of householders were disposed to forego the
status of church membership, and some church members were
satisfied not to assume the responsibilities of the franchise. The
higher offices, such as Magistracies, Governorships and com-
missions in the militia, seldom went begging. In spite of the
lack or inadequacy of the salary, men of estate found that prestige, and the strategy of commerce and land distribution, were
inducements to undertake political service of this sort.

The individual plantation or town started off as a group of
prospective householders having effective possession in common of a tract of land. Ordinarily the original settlers all
shared, though not necessarily equally, in this common ownership. Additional commoners might be admitted for some period
of time after the town was settled. A man might, then, become
a commoner either by being a member of the group which
originally claimed or was granted the town's land or by making
himself acceptable to such a group already in possession. Presumably as long as the commoners considered the gains of additional population and capital to outweigh the scarcity-value
of their existing rights, they would admit newcomers whom
they considered qualified.

At the first settlement, it was customary to divide some proportion of the town's land among the commoners in permanent

private ownership. As the town developed, additional install-
ments were divided from time to time. Some rule of division
had to be found to define the proportionate value of each individual's share. In varying degrees, weight was given to the
size, wealth and social status of each household. Sometimes
contributions to the costs of promotion, such as Indian deeds
and hire of surveyors was considered. Ministers, men of wealth
or political influence, and desirable artisans and tradesmen
found their intangible value to the town reflected to some
degree in the value of their shares.

As the process of division progressed, the practice of adjust-
ing each man's holdings to his apparent needs and capacities
became increasingly formalized until at some point or other the
town was likely to list and tabulate the relative values of existing shares and declare them applicable to all future divisions.

The first division in any town was usually for houselots.
These varied in size both within towns and from town to town,
but one-half acre was a common minimum, and more than ten
or twelve acres larger than ordinary. Houselots were used for
dwelling houses, barns, gardens, small crops and orchards, and
for small livestock. They were laid out along one or a few streets
in a compact plot, the whole frequently fenced or paled against
cattle, wild animals or Indians. The street served as an oc-
casional enclosure for cattle, and as a general-purpose area for
militia training, sawing of timber, storage of wood and bulky
materials, children's play and so forth.

After the division of house lots, the land in the town was
roughly and informally classified as to probable use. As occasion arose, the various classes were either used in common or
reduced to individual ownership. Haying was one of the functions likely to be best carried on individually, and whatever
natural meadow the town had might be divided at an early
stage.[5] Sometimes houselots could be laid out so that some or
all would adjoin their owners' shares of meadow.

5 Plymouth, however, continued for years to hold some meadow as common, dividing the mowing rights each year.

Field crops were grown in common fields similar to the open fields still characteristic of many English villages. The entire field would be surrounded by a single fence, of which each commoner would maintain a number of rods proportionate to the size of his holdings in the field. The town, the selectmen or the owners of the field would then have to decide each year when the field would be opened for cattle to graze on the stubble.

The remainder of the town's land was usually wooded upland used for pasture, timber and fuelwood. Great tracts of such land often remained in common ownership for many years, but the towns divided it piecemeal and some might gradually be converted to more intensive use.

With the houselots and arable fields fenced, the great cattle of the town might simply be turned loose to graze the upland common. This was economical of manpower until the extension of cultivation increased the burden of fencing. It probably wasted stock through loss, poor management and uncontrolled breeding. Commonly, towns provided for herdsmen to tend the cattle on the common. They divided the herd by its functions, reserving the nearby good pasture for milch or draft animals and putting young and dry stock elsewhere. The inner horse- or cow-pastures might be fenced as the fields were. When pasturage, either for the town as a whole or for the inner pasture, became scarce relative to the herd, it might be stinted, the town giving each commoner the right to graze only so many head of specified types of cattle. Some towns had enough pasture so that their commoners could profitably take in cattle from elsewhere for summer feeding, while other towns forbade or limited this practice.

Common pastures and common fields were in a transitional stage between collective and individual ownership. From giving each commoner a share of grazing rights in the pasture it was an easy transition to think of the pasture as their undivided property. In arable fields each individual owned his own plot and had the duty of maintaining a proportionate part of the fence if the town decided to fence the land.[6]

Land which was to be divided was frequently laid out in rectangular units, and each inhabitant given a strip the width of which corresponded to his share. The grants were often measured in acres and rods, and are similar in form to those in English villages where a furlong, or forty rods, was the length of each strip, and therefore one acre would be four rods in width. The form of the survey, therefore, resembled that of the English open field, and the mingling of strips in the New England towns corresponded roughly to the traditional practice at home. But there were differences in organization and land use between the two systems.

Land titles in New England were in fee simple and easily transferable. Individual enclosure and the combination of substantial areas under single ownership were readily accomplished.[7] The two-, three- and four-course rotations of English field systems are not apparent in the colonies. The New England towns grazed their herds for the most part on tracts distinct from the ploughed fields. Therefore the number of the latter depended on topographical convenience rather than (as in England) being equal to the number of years in a complete rotation cycle. Although they adopted the surveying techniques of the mother country, the colonists apparently attempted to arrange things so that divided land could soon be managed by individual owners independently of their neighbors.

These methods of land distribution were adapted to the Puritans' preference for a nucleated form of settlement. They could be used to give each inhabitant a share of each of the kinds of land available. The result was a degree of " zoning " of various kinds of productive activity. The results were more varied and more flexible than the plan of a typical open-field English village, and this greater flexibility was one of the differences

6 Mass. *Records*, I. 215; II, 39, 49; IV-1, 153.

7 Cambridge *Proprietors Records*, 72-116.

which made it possible for New England to avoid the enclosure movement.[8]

Wood was one of New England's abundant and useful resources. Much of the New England forest remained town land, and was available to commoners for use. In many towns growing demand, exhaustion of supply and competition from the need for pasture land led to restrictions on the use of common wood. Strangers and non-commoners were likely to be forbidden to take wood at all. A town might require that dead wood be used for fuel before any live trees were cut. Cutting of firewood or timber for sale out of town was often limited or forbidden.

Many towns required and had inns or ordinaries. These were licensed by the colony or county court on the recommendation of the town, and had a regulated scale of charges. They were not usually subsidized or publicly supported except to the extent that the licensing requirement protected them somewhat from competition. Ferries were established and regulated by town and colony governments. The ferryman was allowed a set scale of charges, usually required to be prepared to provide service whenever demanded, and given a monopoly, sometimes mitigated by a provision that local boat-owners might transport themselves, their neighbors and their property. Towns

8 It was only one of many differences, of course. Another important and fairly obvious one was that the laying of field to field was less likely in a new country to leave anyone short of land.

H. L. Gray, *English Field Systems* (Cambridge, Mass., 1915) describes the types of open-field systems found in England during the several centuries immediately preceding the Puritans' emigration, and reviews briefly the work of other scholars on the same subject. One conclusion of this study is that East Anglia (from which many of New England's colonists came) and other parts of southeast England were more varied and more flexible than the widespread two-field and three-field systems of the midlands.

Melville Eggleston, *The Land System of the New England Colonies* (JHU studies in Historical and Political Science, 4th series, 11, 12, Baltimore, 1886), 36-48, deals with land distribution by New England towns.

Herbert B. Adams, *The Germanic Origin of New England Towns* (same 1st series, 2, Baltimore, 1883) describes the process and endows it with an impressive and questionable genealogy.

not infrequently granted land to ferrymen as an inducement to take up the enterprise.

Water mills were set up on dam sites granted by the colony or town. Their tolls were set at a specified proportion of the meal ground. In addition to water rights, they received grants of land, and sometimes contributions of timber and labor for construction. Some degree of monopoly was frequently provided.

Towns frequently found occasion to offer inducements to men who would practise special skills among them. The ordinary rule of division, by counting the value of a man's trade or profession as part of his estate, served this purpose to some extent. In addition, particularly new or isolated towns might offer additional land or special houselot grants to an artisan on condition that he would ply his trade there.

New England was, of course, everywhere sparsely populated relatively to available resources, by comparison with most inhabited and known regions of that day and this. With no great delay or difficulty, and with no sweeping technological innovations, the region continued for two centuries more or less to absorb additional labor and capital as they presented themselves. In the process, nevertheless, unevenness in population density developed within the region, and people sometimes in some places thought of their own natural environment as niggardly in comparison to what was available at no great distance.

With a few important exceptions, the principal productive operations capable of expansion in New England towns were tillage, livestock production and exploitation of forests. Given the institutional nature of the town, there was a point beyond which further population growth, even with unlimited space, would increase more than proportionately the difficulties in the way of proportionate increase in output. The custom of laying out home lots in a compact settlement made the remoter parts of large towns less available to intensive development. Increases in population, then, would mean less nearby meadow, arable land, pasture and forest for each worker or consumer, and more effort to expend and difficulties to overcome in transporting men, tools and produce to and from the town center. Then too, the quality of land was variable, and a town might grow to the point where the only adjoining vacant land was poorer or more inaccessible than some discontinuous tract. At such a stage of development, the town or its inhabitants might take active steps to transfer a part of the population to new sites or to a remote part of its own land to form a new plantation. Growth in population tended in other words to increase the number rather than the size of communities.

The exhaustibility of local forest resources contributed of course to this tendency. Boston was soon importing firewood and timber from other towns, but Boston was almost unique in that commerce and politics gave her a trade balance vis-a-vis the hinterland that made this possible. Elsewhere, the motivation for some of the town limitations on new house-building seems to have been partly alarm at the inroads being made on timber supplies. We have already seen how some towns restricted wood-cutting and wood-working trades as a conservation measure.

The unoccupied land beyond the frontier offered opportunities for new adventure and income in more than one occupation. Long Island Sound, the Connecticut and Merrimac valleys and the coast and rivers of Maine were explored by traders seeking Indians and the furs they offered in barter. Voyages led to the building of trading posts, which were often forerunners of larger settlements.

Many of these places offered not only fur but marketable wood close to navigation. As the Pilgrims had sent back clapboards in the Mayflower so the early settlers along the Connecticut were soon sending out pipestaves in trade. The wooded rivers and harbors of Maine offered the same resource, and access simultaneously to ship-building materials and productive fishing grounds. Gloucester, Hull and some of the Cape Cod towns were planted by fishermen.

Neither Plymouth nor the Bay towns were established on the best agricultural lands of New England. The Connecticut Valley, central and northern Massachusetts, the land west of Narraganset Bay offered more acres, some of them more fertile, than the increasingly numerous husbandmen of the Bay had to share among themselves closer to home.

Owners of land and houses in the older towns discovered that their property and common rights could be sold at a price to newcomers or ambitious and successful neighbors, and that land and opportunity could be had and developed in newer towns for an outlay chiefly of their own effort and industry. Having hewn out a homestead in a wilderness town once, there were not a few men who were willing to undertake the exciting adventure a second, sometimes a third and fourth time.

As the colonies became settled and permanent communities, the same economic opportunities that had beckoned men across the Atlantic in the first place, now stood as an inducement to follow the advancing fringe of civilization further still. The act of withdrawing from an old social environment to build a new one was an occupation in which men could gain a livelihood and a profit.

There is a certain family resemblance between the process of planting frontier towns and the puritan theories of individual salvation and of church-gathering. Within the old unregenerate man, steeped in sin from the day of Adam's expulsion from Eden, the new man of the spirit struggled against the world, the flesh and the devil for sainthood and salvation. In the midst of the corruptions and innovations of the Church of England, individual Puritans in old and New England sought to regenerate their churches by spiritual mobilization of congregations of individuals assured of their own personal salvation. In withdrawing to New England or to a frontier town, the Puritan could act once more the part of the regenerate man rejecting corrupt institutions, could find one more clean slate on which to inscribe his plan for a pure church in a perfected social order.

CHAPTER II

THE COLONIES' TOWN-PLANTING
POLICIES

COLONIAL governments exercised both political jurisdiction and land ownership throughout New England. The Massachusetts Bay colony had in its charter a grant both of land and of powers of local government, which it interpreted generously during a period when the British government had neither power nor strong inclination to challenge its reading. New Plymouth had a deed of sorts from the Plymouth Company, an inactive English corporate grantee of the territory, but its political constitution rested on a spontaneous assumption of power by its leaders. Connecticut and New Haven based both their land titles and their governing powers largely on effective occupation and exercise, agreement with or conquest of the Indians, and the authority of Scripture and general principles of morality. Rhode Island and Providence plantations did likewise until the hostility of their neighbors led Roger Williams to negotiate for and obtain a colonial charter from the Parliamentary government.

Most of the towns of New England were founded on land granted by one of these colonial governments. As the need for new towns was felt, the colonies devised means of fostering and regulating the process of plantation. Massachusetts undertook a series of surveys, and such towns as Concord, Salisbury, Hampton, Billerica and Haverhill were initiated or encouraged by reports of surveyors to the General Court. The surveyors undertook to estimate the quantity of various classes of land available and the probable human carrying capacity of the site.

A number of the Massachusetts surveys were proposed and initiated by the Colony's General Court. In parts of the colony and in other colonies the initial exploration was done by interested private parties. Merchants, towns, followers of a particular minister and individuals seeking new land were all active in such work.

Most towns were granted to groups of individuals who expressed a desire to settle in them. Usually the grants name a small number, sometimes only one, of those who actually became commoners, and the named grantees then presumably selected additional planters. Occasionally the Massachusetts court appointed a committee to divide lands and admit inhabitants to a new plantation in which the committeemen had no intention of settling.

The earliest Massachusetts towns were on sites preempted without much regard to the possibilities of expansion, and consequently tended to grow into shapes like slabs of a pie with its center at Boston harbor. Boston and Cambridge both found themselves straitened by being largely surrounded by other towns. Where preliminary surveys or grants preceded settlement the tendency was to lay out roughly square or rectangular tracts, often on one or both sides of a stream, with some attempt to include a logical proportion of meadow, arable and upland in the town. Four, six and eight mile squares are found, with varied sizes and shapes in the same general range. Some towns later asked for and received additions, to include a desirable feature which their original bounds were found to leave out; other grants stopped at defined boundaries to leave available a tract which some other future plantation might need.

Such town grants, particularly in Massachusetts, often bore the privilege of exemption from Colony rates for a period usually of three years. In addition, the grantees were called upon to meet conditions within a time limit, failing which the grant would become void. These conditions called for the establishment of a certain number of households (sometimes simply a sufficient number) or of a settled minister or both within a certain number of years.

A number of New England towns were settled on land to which their planters had no formal deed, and consequently had indefinite boundaries and sometimes an uncertain title to their land. All such towns eventually were subjected to the jurisdiction of a colonial government which recognized their title to

their land, and defined its limits. Plymouth grew into a colonial
government itself as towns developed in separate parts of its
land. Massachusetts recognized the claims laid by the Bay
towns of 1630. First Exeter and then the series of settlements
along the Maine coast were annexed by the Massachusetts
colony as it repeatedly reread its charter and resurveyed its
northern boundary.

In Connecticut, the three river towns and the colony sprang
into being about simultaneously, as the representatives of the
towns early met together to establish the colony's bounds and
frame a general government. The colony of Rhode Island and
Providence plantations consisted of four towns which were
established and functioned for some time independently. In
spite of differences among themselves, they ultimately submitted to a sort of federated colony government. The town of
New Haven early produced a series of offshoot towns, and
entered into cooperative arrangements with other independent
plantations in the region. The result was another colonial government, more or less federal in origin, which was extinguished
when Connecticut, under the Royal charter of 1662, annexed
its member towns.

Massachusetts granted slightly less than 100,000 acres to
individuals directly, consisting of land not included in town
grants. Connecticut made colonial grants in smaller number
and extent. A large number of the Massachusetts grants were
in return for investment in the original stock of the Massachusetts Bay Company, at the rate of 100 acres for each £25 subscribed and paid in. Such grants continued to be made practically to the end of the life of the original Company's charter
in 1692. Apparently rather than making a general distribution
based on the Company records, the General Court permitted
individual stockholders to come in at their leisure, prove their
claims and receive individual grants. Both Massachusetts and
Connecticut rewarded certain individuals for their services in
the colonies' militia with land, and both remunerated some of
the services of civilian magistrates and officers of government

by the same means. John Winthrop, after a moving recital of the losses and burdens he had assumed as Governor of Massachusetts, received a thousand-acre farm in Medford; Thomas Dudley, his Lieutenant-Governor and sometime Governor, another generous tract. Captain John Mason, hero of the Pequot war, was given five hundred acres of his conquest by the Connecticut General Court, and a hundred acres apiece for five of his comrades in arms. The Massachusetts commissioners who negotiated for the submission of the Maine settlements were compensated in acreage for that service.

Enterprise of various kinds was rewarded and encouraged with colony land grants. The promoters of the iron works at Lynn and Braintree received iron ore and fuelwood grants. John Winthrop, Jr., was active in securing these concessions, and obtained a large tract including a deposit of graphite or plumbago which he proposed to mine. Proprietors and promoters of saltworks were subsidized by land grants, and timber-bearing acreage given to projectors of saw-mills. In a few cases the honorable destitution of families whose members had performed public service was relieved by gratuities in the form of colony lands.

There is evident in these individual land grants a certain lack of system and consistent policy. A fixed ratio between the subscriptions of adventurers in company stock and acreage granted was maintained, but it was left to individuals to prove their claims and get the ear of the General Court, when and how they saw fit. No orderly principles are discernible by which the size of other grants was proportioned to the value of the services rewarded, and it is obvious that many honorable veterans of public service both military and civil never claimed or obtained rewards in this form. One is left with the impression that this practice was a means of quieting the pleas of demanding or influential individuals rather than a settled part of the colonial system of land distribution.

Most of these grants in their original form were for a given acreage, undefined or very loosely defined as to location or boundaries. If and when an individual wanted to exercise his claim, the General Court usually authorized him or a surveyor to lay out and bound the tract. Upon receiving the report of the survey, the court would formally vest the ownership of the tract in the grantee. Until the last stage was reached, the grantee was privileged to change his mind, withdraw his claim to the tract in question, and hunt out another that he liked better. Massachusetts at one time threatened to void grants that were not laid out within three years, but this was apparently not enforced, and at the end of the period under consideration there was a substantial acreage of unsurveyed claims against the unappropriated land of the colony.

The land brought under private ownership by this system was not ordinarily included within towns. Often the grants contained the provision that they were not to prejudice the laying out of any present or future plantation. Occasionally a grantee would add together a colony grant and a town common right and take them as part of the town's division. Winthrop's Medford farm was occupied and operated independently of adjoining towns, but partially subordinated to Charlestown in matters of civil government. Saltonstall Park, east of the river near Windsor, Connecticut, was more or less absorbed by its neighbor town, with some recognition of the owner's claims. Some of the other grants were occasionally or regularly occupied and used independently of any town government. The veterans' lands in the Pequot country became the nucleus of a plantation which grew into a town. For the most part, such lands as were occupied by permanent households were absorbed by towns or grew into towns themselves. But for our period, this method of land distribution and settlement was an exception rather than the rule, and accounted for a minute proportion of the whole process of plantation.

A plantation without a church and a settled minister, and without a prospect of getting one, had a pretty poor outlook for survival. Massachusetts often required that the promoters of a new town settle twenty families, or a sufficient number of families, and a minister before the grant became final. In general, such requirements were satisfactorily met, and the supply of planters and ministers was adequate to sustain a continued advance of the frontier. Sometimes, however, a plantation site went begging for a short while, or failed for a time to attract and hold a sufficient population. Shawshin was offered as a town site several times, before Cambridge planted there the village which later became the town of Billerica. The first grantees of Lancaster failed to populate the town sufficiently and the General Court intervened, appointing commissioners to reorganize the settlement. Eastham on Cape Cod languished, was abandoned and was later taken up by another group. Saybrook for a while was a mere fort, with a small garrison, until a company of settlers found it attractive.

The general purpose of town grants was to get households properly established and the land effectively utilized. The centralized town plot and the customary institutions of church and civil government were regarded as essential, and the grants made in such a form as to encourage and require their development. Massachusetts enforced for a while a law forbidding the occupation of dwellings more than half a mile from a meeting house, Plymouth prosecuted for disorderly living some men who chose to dwell in isolated homes, and in general the single house alone in open country was discouraged as presenting special problems of defense and social morality. Where remote houses existed, they were sometimes used as seasonal dwellings for cultivators of outlying farms. Such farms might sometimes develop into a settlement that became a village, eventually acquiring its own minister and public officials and the status of a town.

Most towns included at least some freemen; where they did not, special problems of local government arose. The freemen elected, and were qualified to serve as selectmen, constables, jurors, deputies to the General Court and magistrates. To some extent they had a preferred status as commoners and in land divisions, although freemen and non-freemen alike shared common rights in most towns, and had a voice in some of the decisions about land management.

The colonial government required that one of the inhabitants of each town serve as constable, acting for both the town and the colony in law-enforcement and collection and custody of taxes. Massachusetts towns were expected to send two deputies apiece to the General Court twice a year, although some towns repeatedly failed to do so. A town distant from Boston might economize by naming a non-resident as deputy. When the Colony's court of magistrates proved inadequate, county courts were established, and commissioners for small causes appointed for localities where they were needed.

The men of each town were organized as a unit of militia, and trained and commanded by militia officers, of whom the principal ones were commissioned by the colonial General Courts.

The freemen in each town elected a large number of local officials, who served on a part-time basis as selectmen, town clerks, surveyors of town lands and roads, fence-viewers and field drivers for the common fields, and so forth. Service in most of these offices was compulsory, and many freemen and some non-freemen must have borne a considerable burden of public duties. Perhaps because men whose rated estates were large were regarded as best fitted for public office, or perhaps because their political position gave them an advantage, the class of men who performed public duties were on the whole generously treated in land divisions.

Men who were admitted to towns as inhabitants shared, if they arrived early enough, in the town's land. Otherwise they were permitted to purchase land and common rights from former owners. Normally it was expected of them to occupy and cultivate the land. This condition was sometimes made explicit, and some men's common rights lapsed when they failed to exercise them. They bore the obligation of paying town and colony rates, which might be settled in kind, and of performing public service when called upon. The New England frontiersman of the Puritan era lived in a community in which, however new it was, he enjoyed the advantages and bore the responsibilities of a member of an established social order.

To be admitted as an inhabitant in a town, a man had to demonstrate himself worthy of the status. Some degree of property, valuable skill or industriousness was expected of him, as well as good behavior as a citizen and (except in Providence and the Rhode Island colony) freedom from active heresy in religion. Lacking these qualifications, he might be compelled to an ordered mode of life either as a householder or as a servant, barred or expelled from the town or banished from the colony altogether.

People who were neither heads nor subordinate members of recognized households were referred to as sojourners. In Massachusetts, their presence had to be reported to the selectmen within three weeks, and they could stay beyond that period only by permission. Other colonies and their towns controlled such sojourners in similar ways.

Much of the motivation for the control of sojourners came from the town's obligation under the poor law to relieve destitution among its own residents. Newcomers who arrived as servants, laborers, transient tradesmen or visitors might be required to find householders who would bind themselves to relieve the town of such liability. Or they might be required to enter contracts for a year or more of service to some responsible employer as a condition of being permitted to remain in town.

New England towns and colonies were in the nature of private associations in that they carefully controlled admission to membership in the community and in its various estates and ranks. This was done as a part of the general scheme for making the social structure of the colonies conform to desired standards of social order. Orthodoxy, industriousness and success as a producer would find a man a place in the social order; habitual idleness, heresy or unwillingness to accept his assigned

role in the established order of things would make him a misfit
to be authoritatively put in his place or forcibly banished.

Most New Englanders accepted uncritically or staunchly
supported the immemorial tradition that provision of a system
of religious worship and instruction, preservation of its orthodoxy and repression of heresy by both didactic and punitive
means was a public function ranking in importance with the
preservation of law and order through political institutions.
The church in the New England town was, then, a public service, benefitting every soul in town. To the unregenerate it
offered instruction and exhortation designed to guide them on
the path to salvation. To the apparently sanctified it offered a
sacramental rite and moral guidance to preserve them from the
assaults of the forces of evil. Attendance at its public exercises
and acceptance of its doctrines was as much a universal duty
as obedience to law and public authority. Probably the ordinary run of colonists never seriously questioned this tradition.
The Puritan leaders presented it as the primitive and Scriptural form of the church, opposing what they described as the
arbitrary introduction of innovations and the inventions of men
into the worship of God practised by Archbishop Laud and
their opponents in the hierarchy of the English church. A substantial number of their followers listened, learned and found a
satisfying religious experience in the churches they gathered.
How many were apathetic, and how many conformed because
they would conform to anything not drastically unfamiliar, we
do not know. How many swallowed an unpleasant doctrine in
return for the privilege of scratching a livelihood from the New
England frontier, historians have debated with no entirely
clear result. But in the first four decades of colonization, the
overwhelming majority of planters accepted with varying degrees of enthusiasm life under the assumption that to attend
regular services in an orthodox church, to hear weekly instruction in and exposition of its doctrines, to make appropriate
material contribution to its support and the maintenance of its

clergy was as much a part of his duty as to obey the law and keep civil peace.

Those who through an inward experience of regeneration learned themselves, and through public confession and outward righteousness demonstrated to the congregation that they were of the elect, were full-fledged communicating members of the church. The classical Calvinist position was that election was a foreordained act of Divine omnipotence, that individuals were born and conceived either saved or damned and that whether or not one was a good Christian was beyond the power of an individual's will to determine. Those who were saved probably behaved like good moral and pious men. Those who were damned probably behaved like rascals. But a rascal might turn out to be saved and start acting like a saint, and an outwardly moral man might turn out to be damned and all his good behavior would not stand him in stead. The foundation of the Puritan minister's moral and rhetorical power lay in the Scriptural and philosophical learning which enabled him to teach his congregation how to recognize the biddings and promptings of good and evil in their own breasts. He warned the outward saints that there might be that evil within them that would plunge them into irredeemable sin. In the face of such warnings they were likely to search their souls hopefully for motives that would make their outward behavior evidence an inner sanctity. To the unregenerate the minister held out the hope that they might yet be saved, and they carefully nurtured anything in their own thoughts and conduct that might prove to be the workings of salvation.

Thus the keys of the kingdom of heaven, which the Reformation had wrenched from the hands of St. Peter's successors, were in effect put under the unacknowledged guardianship of the Puritan clergy. And thus the churches of New England were a vital and powerful part of the battery of techniques designed to direct the life of the individual according to the standards of the social group of which he was a member.

Puritan moral philosophy had a tendency to produce its own backfires. It invited the non-conformist to claim that his was the pathway to salvation and that the established order might lead into the pitfalls of error and evil. We shall see shortly that at times such questionings of the validity of Puritan orthodoxy were facilitated by and encouraged the active development of the Puritan frontier.

One of the issues which aroused controversy was that of infant baptism. Whatever the symbolism involved, members of Christian communities were in the habit of having their children baptised at an early age, and the desire for this service persisted in the popular mind. But strict congregationalists refused to administer this sacrament to the children of men and women who were not themselves communicating members of churches. From this position one natural course of development led to Antipedobaptism, another to accepting the children of those who, though not visibly regenerate, were reasonably respectable and orthodox in belief. Each of these tendencies toward heresy was on occasion a divisive influence.[1]

The material needs of the Puritan church were a legitimate charge against the community it served. Every town in New England, except the heretical and tolerant plantations of Rhode Island, Providence and Warwick, included church expenses, the largest ordinarily being the minister's salary, among the public purposes for which it raised funds by taxation. Governor Winthrop at one point, and some others, may have felt that in principle voluntary contributions were more desirable, but where voluntary contributions fell short, they conceded that a rate would have to be imposed by the town.[2]

The ministerial rate gave rise to controversy. Those who objected to the validity of the ministry or the correctness of the doctrine preached laid themselves open, of course, to a charge of heresy, and recanted, departed or were treated as common

1 See Chapter V below.

2 Winthrop *Journal*, I, 114, 299.

criminals. But in a few cases where two congregations shared the services of a minister, and in several where a part of a town wished to withdraw to create its own congregation and call its own minister, financial problems tended to complicate a situation which might present other difficulties.

The official attitude toward the planting of towns developed into a fairly clear and consistent policy. Frontier individualism was restrained by making the town, rather than the isolated farm, the unit of plantation. Large urban aggregations were not rapidly developed, as circumstances and policy combined to distribute the growing population into new towns. The Puritan leaders had a plan for an ordered form of civil society, a philosophy setting forth the relationship between God, man and the community, and a propaganda system by which the plan and the philosophy were presented to the general public in a way designed to secure their assent and sustain their cooperative effort. They cast their policies in a mold designed to adapt familiar and desired forms of institutions to the task of subduing a wilderness.

CHAPTER III

THE DISCOVERY OF THE FRONTIER

TOWN-PLANTING was not an easy procedure for the Puritans to learn. Frontier conditions were new to the colonists at first, and they had few guides to the wilderness in which they found themselves. Differences of opinion and of personal bent developed, and the exodus to a new town might start with sometimes a tearful and sometimes an angry parting. The problem of adapting the size and resources of a town to its people and functions was dealt with by trial and error. No usefully accurate forecast of rates of immigration and population growth could be attempted with the means at hand. The decision to adventure one's family and estate in the wilderness led not only to an upheaval in ordinary modes of living and working, but to an active and dynamic development of emotional and intellectual experience. The incoming colonial population included a large proportion of educated men [1] who were in the habit of conveying their ideas to the general public, and many of its ordinary people were in the habit of listening to and studying the teachings of a learned ministry, so that the problems were generally discussed and debated.

From the planting of the seven Bay towns in 1630 until 1634 the only new plantation within Massachusetts was Ipswich. The other towns, meanwhile, were gaining in population to the point where some accommodation for the increased numbers must be found. In 1635, with somewhat the air of taking a plunge, a company of planters pushed inland to Concord. This first essay at plantation beyond the head of navigation was encouraged by tax exemption and by a grant of authority to press carts for transportation. In the same year Hingham and Newbury were started, and twenty-one families permitted to revive the old settlement of Weymouth. The General Court ordered a

1 S. E. Morison, in *The Puritan pronaos*, estimates that the proportion was substantially above that found either in seventeenth-century England or in modern America.

survey of the tract that was to become Andover, and announced that it was available for settlement. Dedham was laid out and settled in 1636, Billerica offered but not accepted, and Hampton, granted in that year, was settled in 1639. With the granting of Gloucester and Salisbury in 1639, Massachusetts had in ten years of active existence launched an active program of expanding settlement.

The Puritan minister Ezekiel Rogers arrived in 1638 with a company of settlers who had followed him from his English parish. The next spring the General Court granted the group a tract they had left vacant when Salem, Ipswich and Newbury were bounded, on which the town of Rowley was planted. John Davenport's prospective congregation, at about the same time, presented a similar problem which was resolved when they later chose a site beyond the colony's borders.

During the same decade several of the original towns accommodated part of their own population on dependent but separate plantations which were called villages. Cambridge and Dorchester made divisions of their own outlying land among their commoners on which were planted the beginnings of villages which would later become the towns of Newton and Milton. Boston in 1634 obtained land at Mount Wollaston and Muddy River which, divided, became settlements destined to become Braintree and Brookline. Cambridge and Charlestown were both offered the tract then called Shawshin, but refused for the time being. In 1637 some Watertown commoners, petitioning the General Court for more land, were given a tract on which they planted Sudbury. Within a few years following Salem, Lynn, Charlestown and Cambridge had all produced offshoots of this sort, and the tendency for growing towns to reproduce their kind by expansion and division persisted long past the end of our period.

Massachusetts was designed as an orderly civilized community in a day when religious diversity and civil disobedience were virtually indistinguishable. But the orthodoxy of the Puritans was to be maintained through public exhortation and exposition by a learned ministry. Modern interpreters are likely to think of it as an official body of social theory sustained by a propaganda machine. To the Puritans, though, truth was something to be discovered and then defended by what we would regard as both fair means and foul. Truth could be discovered by reading the Word of God and interpreting the events of the world with the aid of the analytical tools available to scholarly men. A body of learned ministers should be able to agree among themselves and with a Christian magistracy.as to the best attainable form of Church and Civil Government.

Such agreement among the ministry was not always attainable. When learned, well-intentioned and respectable men reached different conclusions the result more than once was a withdrawal to a new plantation on the frontier by one of the parties. The first time this happened was when Roger Williams moved to Providence in the winter of 1635-1636. Williams had arrived in New England in 1631, had preached in the churches of Plymouth and Salem and had engaged in trade with the Indians. At Salem in 1633 and 1634 he had begun to argue that the churches in England were no true churches, that neither the British Crown nor the colonists under its protection could have a legal title to New England land except by purchase from the Indians, and that civil magistrates could not lawfully punish breaches of the first four commandments. These beliefs were not tolerable to the main body of Massachusetts Puritans. They were interested in purifying the established churches both in old and New England, not in initiating a rival ecclesiastical structure. Although they often bought out the Indian claims to territory they occupied, they did so as a convenient way of gaining unchallenged possession of that which was their own by royal grant. And the idea that such desirable things as religious truth and unity of worship should not be sustained and defended by political power they simply did not comprehend.

Williams therefore was a threat to the established order of things. His arguments challenged some of the theoretical foundations of Puritan institutions. To tolerate him would be, furthermore, an admission that reasonable men might lawfully hold differing views on fundamental issues. After debate and political pressure had failed to change his views, Williams was sentenced to banishment from the colony and avoided deportation to England by making his way to Narraganset Bay. Here he purchased land from the Indians and was joined by twelve associates, with whom he founded the plantation of Providence.

The new town, like Plymouth before and like others later, derived its governing powers from a plantation covenant in which the inhabitants agreed to " subject ourselves . . . to all such orders or agreements as shall be made for the public good of the body . . . by the major consent of the present inhabitants, masters of families . . . and others whom they shall admit unto them. . . . " [2] In admitting new inhabitants, dividing lands and using their commons, Providence behaved much as other New England towns. One group of inhabitants aroused controversy by purchasing a tract of land called Pawtuxit and refusing to share it with other commoners.

Providence had a church, which became Separatist and then Baptist. But the inhabitants agreed to tolerate differences of opinion, and there were always dissenters. Williams himself eventually doubted the validity of his own rebaptism, and seems to have come to the belief that none of the traditional sacraments were surely grounded on adequate authority.

Here, then, was a plantation arising out of a difference of opinion. The planting of Providence demonstrated that diversity of beliefs could develop without destroying the framework of New England society and without requiring the Puritans to abandon their attempt to maintain an orthodox system of theology and church government.

2 Rhode Island *Records*, I, 14.

In 1636 and 1637 a considerable body of Bostonians had developed a line of thought which orthodox Puritans generally denounced under the name of Antinomianism. This heresy maintained that the Holy Spirit dwelt in the soul of a regenerate Christian. But if it was this indwelling that served as evidence of election, what incentive remained to outward sanctity of behavior? The Puritan ministry had carefully evolved out of the Calvinist doctrine that those who were saved would behave well willy-nilly the argument that he who wanted to be saved had better behave well. Antinomians emphasized God's Grace as the source of salvation, held that an individual might surely recognize the workings of Grace within himself, and that such an individual was above and beyond the workings of the moral law. This seemed to orthodox ministers and magistrates to undermine the theological foundations of law, government and morality altogether.

Among the members of the Antinomian party, Ann Hutchinson was brought to a spectacular and well-remembered trial at which the magistrates banished her from Massachusetts. John Wheelwright, one of the ministers of Boston, was found to be tainted with the heresy and condemned to exile. Numerous members of the party were ordered disarmed, and several of them given permission to leave the jurisdiction and an official intimation that they had better do so. Sixteen men who had been subjected to such action were among the nineteen who signed the first covenant at Portsmouth, R. I., on the 7th of March 1638.[3] A year later, after newcomers had increased the population of Portsmouth substantially, the plantation divided, many of the original settlers and others taking up land at another part of the Island to found Newport.

Wheelwright chose to lead another group of Antinomians to Exeter, where they planted a town and signed a covenant on unclaimed land. In 1643 the Bay colony, having surveyed the northern boundary of its grant, claimed that Exeter fell within its jurisdiction and annexed the town. Wheelwright

3 Rhode Island *Records*, I, 52.

moved on to Wells on the Maine coast, where a few years later
he found a verbal formula whereby he could reconcile himself
with official Massachusetts Puritanism.

Except for Warwick, R. I., where in 1642 a group of ex-
ceptionally imaginative and individualistic Puritan rebels
planted a town which was to become part of the Rhode Island
colony, these cases complete the tale of the outcast heretical
plantations of Puritan New England. Later breaches were
healed by reconciliation, or by removal and new plantations
before the penalties of law were invoked. Beginning about 1660
a few sectarian or dissident congregations won grudging toleration.

These outbursts of anger at parting were, of course, part of
the evolution of law and political philosophy whereby colonies
with established churches grew into the America of the First
Amendment. Coming as they did in the earliest days of New
England expansion, they may also be growing pains incident
to the development of a program of plantation. In 1630 the Assistants had misgivings about pushing the frontier as far back
as Ipswich. Williams, Wheelwright and the Rhode Islanders
demonstrated dramatically the existence and value of available plantation sites beyond the immediate hinterland of the
Bay.

One fertile, attractive and commercially valuable region
where Massachusetts assisted the process of putting the land
into friendly hands was the Connecticut Valley. Both the Dutch
from New Amsterdam and the Plymouth colony had trading
houses on the river. One group of noble and wealthy English
Puritans had a patent to the area and seemed on the point of
dividing it into manor-like grants on which they could establish themselves as a sort of colonial gentry. The river promised
a large and flourishing Indian trade and even a potential rival
to the St. Lawrence and the Hudson as a pathway to the un-
known interior of the continent. The land it watered was soon
recognized for what it still is, a valley notably well-adapted by
nature to tillage in a region where such natural endowment is
in general not over-generous.

The people who planted the first towns on the Connecticut were from four of the original Massachusetts Bay towns. Dorchester and Cambridge churches and ministers moved lock, stock and barrel, taking about one-third of Dorchester's population and a large proportion of Cambridge's. Watertown and Roxbury experienced sizable withdrawals, and the four river towns bore at first the same four names. Governor Winthrop reported, after discussing the matter with Cambridge men in 1634, that: " The principal reasons for their removal were,

" 1. Their want of accomodation for their cattle, so as they were not able to maintain their ministers, nor could receive any more of their friends to help them; and here it was alleged by Mr. Hooker, as a fundamental error, that towns were set so near to each other.

" 2. The fruitfulness and commodiousness of Connecticut, and the danger of having it possessed by others, Dutch or English.

" 3. The strong bent of their spirits to remove thither." [4]

It was urged upon them that " being knit to us in one body," they ought not to depart, that division would weaken all the plantation, that land nearer home was available. The General Court invited them to find another plantation site on the Merrimac or elsewhere in the colony,[5] offered them Boston's land at Muddy River if Hooker's church would stay,[6] but in 1635 the would-be emigrants in Cambridge and the other towns were sending advance parties to the Connecticut [7] and in 1636 the Massachusetts colony commissioned a temporary government for the plantation there.[8]

Several motives may be discerned for the decision to move made by the Connecticut planters. In Cambridge for some years

4 Winthrop, *Journal*, I, 132.

5 Mass. *Records*, I, 119.

6 Mass. *Records*, I, 129.

7 Winthrop, *Journal*, I, 163.

8 Mass. *Records*, I, 170-171.

afterward evidence continued to appear that the lands of the town were an inconvenient size and shape, and it seemed difficult to arrange the population in a form of settlement that would comfortably support town and church activities. The early settlers of Dorchester were largely from the western counties of Devon and Dorset, and had come as a group, not entirely mingled with the East Anglian colonists in the other towns. This separateness, and the increasing number of relative strangers seeking homes in the town, may have tended to make these planters into a cohesive and mobile group ready to respond to a demonstration of the advantages of a new site. William Pynchon of Roxbury was interested in the Indian trade, and persuaded a number of neighbors to associate with him for the move. Thomas Hooker, pastor of the Cambridge church, was at the time of his departure under heavy verbal fire from the Antinomians, as being a man who walked in a covenant of works. He may well have felt that physical withdrawal from proximity to his opponents' stronghold of Boston would contribute to ecclesiastical harmony.

The condition that made the Connecticut settlement economically possible was the growing population in Eastern Massachusetts, and the availability of resources and commercial opportunities in the valley. In the Puritan plan the project was an outpost against rivals, a means of planting new churches and a device whereby a theological disagreement of low intensity could be made to contribute to the growth of the Puritan community without impairing its unity.

In 1635 and 1636 the river towns of Wethersfield, Hartford, Windsor and Springfield were exporting a few furs and a little lumber, but were still far short of self-sufficiency in their food supply. In 1637 their new colonial government maintained a force of militiamen in the Pequot war, in which with the help of Massachusetts they acquired a claim by conquest to a substantial tract of land usable for their expanding settlements. Before long the new colony was competing with New Haven for town sites on Long Island Sound and laying the groundwork for new towns in the valley.

While the Bay colony was gaining population in the years following 1630, Plymouth shared its growth. By 1640 Duxbury was a separate town, and Marshfield on its way to becoming one, both peopled by an overflow from Plymouth. Settlers from Weymouth and elsewhere in Massachusetts had crossed the border in sufficient numbers to found a town at Scituate in 1638. Taunton and the Cape Cod towns of Yarmouth, Barnstable and Sandwich were planted by organized companies from Massachusetts in 1638 and 1639.

Northeast of Newbury and Hampton, a fringe of coastal and river settlements was growing independently of the Puritan colonies. Dover had some inhabitants in 1632, and there was probably more than one small settlement beyond within the next few years. Robert Gorges, an English claimant to the area, attempted to promote plantations in the region. His claims were opposed by Massachusetts Bay, which also used a threat of military action to discourage French penetration. Traders from New Plymouth maintained a trucking house on the Penobscot.

During the 1640's and 1650's the Bay colony reinterpreted its charter boundaries. The north line was to be three miles north of Merrimac River. This, it was decided, should mean a parallel of latitude three miles north of the river's northernmost point, extended from sea to sea. Successive explorations followed the course of the river further and further north, and successive boundary revisions pushed the jurisdiction of Massachusetts on until by 1660 it had swept unopposed through coastal New Hampshire and much of Maine. These settlements were, some of them, far from being of an unadulterated Puritanism, but the Massachusetts leaders seemed to regard their annexation as the safe and desirable course, even when some compromise of colonial orthodoxy was part of the price.

The first decade of population growth, somewhat to the surprise of the Puritan leaders, produced an expansion of the area of plantation and a marked decentralization of social institutions, which took the form of a rapid multiplication of towns. The arrival of newcomers in older communities led to social pressures which gradually or abruptly, amicably or otherwise divided the social organism into two groups, one of whom sought a frontier site where it could withdraw from the other. We may at this point attempt a general description and classification of patterns of growth and division typical of this process.

The New England plantation and town of the seventeenth century presents an interesting problem in the economics of optimum size. So long as natural, political or ideological circumstances combined to impose the condition of a compact plat of houselots on the community, more residents would mean a longer average distance from the houselot to adequate supplies of arable and meadow land, pasture, fuel and timber. The choice, for junior claimants to the common land, lay between cultivating small allotments intensively and undertaking a long daily journey to remote parts of town. A natural impulse, under the circumstances, was to arrange dwelling accommodations at the remote division. An isolated house so situated was called a farm house. Often, apparently, it was only seasonally occupied. When several adjacent farms were built in a compact group the settlement was called a village. From farm or village men, women and children had to make the weekly journey to their town for the Sabbath-day meeting. Householders and freemen transacted town and colony business at a distance. Militiamen might be called away on training days to leave their affairs untended and their homes unguarded.

Villagers tended to demand a degree of independence from the central town which would enable them to avoid this burden of travel. Often their first move was to hire their own preacher and hold church services at the village. This, though it appeared on the surface to have none but praiseworthy effects, was expensive—in a day when grains were bringing a few shillings a bushel, a preacher might reasonably demand £50 to £100 as his annual salary. The villagers would understandably request to be relieved from the double taxation involved if they contributed locally for the village minister while paying town rates which were used to maintain the central church. Repeatedly this type of problem led to litigation before the General Court, which leaned somewhat toward upholding the villagers, but often delayed a final settlement of the issue until a good deal of fuming had gone on. Once having won the right to its own church meetings, the village progressed often without serious obstruction to the acquisition of its own local officials, its own militia troop and its own local rates, and finally attained the status of an independent town.

English Puritanism was a political opposition party and a revolutionary movement. In the face of official opposition it had an ideological unity which was lost on both the occasions when it acquired political power. In England the Puritan Revolution of 1642-1660 revealed insuperable difficulties besetting the attempt to base a political program on a system of doctrinal orthodoxy. In New England the Puritan colonies preserved orthodoxy by making the frontier a dumping ground on which the weeds of heresy were cast out and grew. Providence, Portsmouth, Newport, Exeter and Warwick provided outlets for human energies which under other circumstances might have produced a proliferation of dissenting sects. Heresy was endemic, relatively harmless and only partially checked in some of the remote plantations of Cape Cod. In Connecticut doctrinal differences from the Massachusetts position could persist without seriously breaching the friendly relations between the two colonies, and Connecticut's dissenters could amicably withdraw across the colony line to plant Hadley. Ultimately the settled communities in New England learned to adapt themselves to variations in belief among their members, but for many years breaches in doctrinal unity were among the divisive tendencies leading to new plantation.

Immigrants to the New England colonies frequently arrived in more or less cohesive groups, usually centered around a minister. The Massachusetts grant to Ezekiel Rogers and his prospective church placed one such group in its own town of Rowley. John Davenport, having preached in the heart of commercial London, developed a following of merchants and tradesmen who joined with him in planting New Haven. Steven Batchelor and Richard Blinman both led small bands of followers from town to town before their flock established a permanent home. As long as ministers continued to arrive from England new plantations served as a means of supporting them and providing space and a livelihood for their audiences.

Experience soon indicated (although it was not necessarily good law) that permanent occupation and use were, for Englishmen, the usual prelude to a legally defensible title to land. Except for the aborigines settled populations were not and have not since been displaced in the region in any great numbers, and local political institutions have evolved without very sudden drastic changes. The colonial leaders, therefore, had a fairly strong inducement to permit and encourage the acquisition and occupation of land by planters under their jurisdiction or friendly to them. Massachusetts fostered the eastward extension of its settlements partly to forestall and repel French and British rivals, and the planting of its own Connecticut Valley and its alliance with the Connecticut and New Haven colonies drove back the Dutch and later helped limit the eastern extension of the boundaries of New York. One attempt to plant a Massachusetts town near Fort Orange on the Hudson came to naught, and as neither the Connecticut nor the Merrimac commanded a western gateway, the Middle West escaped direct political and commercial domination by New England. But the Puritans made the attempt, and in the area which they claimed and occupied, their land titles and some of their political institutions have resisted external encroachments.

Individual seekers of profit first of all directed their attention to trade in fish and furs. As the colonies grew, it became

profitable to deal in the products and needs of the settlers, and
industries such as wood-working, ship-building and iron-mak-
ing developed. Some business men took a direct interest in the
process of plantation. William and John Pynchon devoted
much work to the settlement of the upper Connecticut Valley,
and maintained a successful trade in its products. John Oldham
explored Long Island Sound and the Connecticut River in his
fur-gathering trips, and was interested in the plans for the Connecticut migration when on a trading voyage he was killed by
Indians in 1633. The younger John Winthrop participated in
the planting of a number of towns scattered from Ipswich to
New Haven. These enterprisers took their gains in often generous town land allotments and in opportunities for commercial
profit. Political office was sometimes a reward for or the pathway to their achievements. They organized the process of plantation, saw themselves the economic contrast between the
values of settled and virgin land and served in some instances
to imbue potential planters with a sense of this contrast.

The Puritan design for frontier development was never a
blueprint complete to the last nailhole. The process seems to
have been not entirely free of surprises to anyone involved.
But throughout the Puritan period some elements of a plan are
apparent. Men should live in a settled social order. Next above
the family in the table of organization stands the plantation,
which is a unit designed to support a gathered church and
which has political, productive and land-managing functions on
the same scale. The foundation of churches and of civil society,
we are repeatedly told and shown, is a covenant in which men
agree together to a generally advantageous subordination of
constituted authority. Covenants are actually used to establish
churches, towns, colonies and for simpler purposes such as
ordering the maintenance of common fences. There is a Divine
law and a Divine order of social institutions, and the way to
build it is by the voluntary common submission of groups of
Christians to its decrees.

Covenant-making was a valuable skill for people developing a frontier of towns. It gave authority and self-assurance to groups of planters, and was the institutional foundation of social cooperation in frontier communities. It served to sustain the position of magistrates and church leaders in established settlements, and met the needs of dissenting groups for an organizational outlet for their energies. There were some good geographical reasons why seventeenth century New England nurtured neither the isolated frontier farms of the nineteenth century West nor the plantations of one family and its servants of the southern colonies. But the Puritans' secure possession of a theory of social order adaptable to the circumstances of New England life must have had an important effect on the form which their colonial development took.

The Puritan plantation was not a democracy, and it was not communist. Although the theory of the covenant contained the idea of voluntary submission to authority, the laws to which people submitted recognized a system of social status. Among the advantages of civil (as opposed to natural) liberty was the orderly division of functions in which men of wealth, learning, ability and proven sanctity were given a greater burden of responsibility and a greater share of the political rights and economic opportunity they needed to shoulder the burden. Governor Winthrop was fond of the metaphor of the body politic, in which the head and the higher and lower members all had assigned positions and functions and worked together best when they avoided mutual interference. He and others classified three possible forms of government—monarchy, aristocracy, democracy. Either of the first two was a sound and usable political structure, but for democracy most articulate seventeenth-century New Englanders found no warrant in Scripture or in reason. Even in Providence, where the word democracy was less repulsive than elsewhere, the plantation covenant submitted its signers to such orders as should be made " by the major consent of the present inhabitants, masters of families . . . and others whom they shall admit unto them." [9]

9 Rhode Island *Records*, I, 14.

The broadest electorates to be found in the colonies were still restricted by the requirement of formal admission.

Government and economic life were, then, based on a fairly numerous aristocracy with a series of gradations. The ministry enjoyed a near monopoly of the function of disseminating ideas to the community in general. Magistrates, called to office by the electorate, were nonetheless charged with the duty of enforcing a system of law which stood above and beyond the control of the popular will. There were those of them who argued that it was wrong of the freemen to turn any man out of elective office without proven charges of misconduct. Freemen constituted a carefully selected minority of the adult men of the colony. Within the towns, inhabitants were admitted under selective tests of wealth and worth, and their share in the town's affairs and land was proportioned to their family size, estate, training and social standing.

Though a large proportion of the productive work of a plantation might take place on common land and through some degree of collective action, there was no indiscriminate pooling of tasks or possessions. Individual inhabitants always held defined and calculable property rights in the town commons. Taxes and the obligations of public service were distributed among them according to definite principles. Within the plantation the aim was to balance individual contributions and individual rewards. Throughout New England this led in practise to a fairly expeditious and systematic distribution of a large proportion of town common lands to private owners. And the value of the individual's claim against the group was proportioned to some social estimate of the worth of the individual.

This system and theory of social order was readily adaptable to the planting of new towns. When one or more of the influences making for a willingness to migrate was present, people had not only access to vacant and virtually free land but also an established habit and method of organization which they could use to reduce it to usefulness.

PART II

TOWN PLANTING AS A TECHNIQUE OF FRONTIER DEVELOPMENT

CHAPTER IV

GROWTH OF TOWNS

THE various kinds of influences that impelled individuals and groups to the decision to plant new towns are described in this and the following chapters. The groups and plantations selected for more extended description are, I hope, a reasonable sample of cases in which the town-planting tendency may be studied in some detail. These cases are classified as responses to the needs and desires of growing towns, of religious dissenters, of newly-arrived ministers and of individuals and groups simply seeking economic success. Broad as these categories are, many plantations might with little strain be fitted into more than one of them. But they are a useful frame in which to display some illustrative examples of the workings of the town-planting process.

Most of the towns planted on unoccupied soil in the seventeenth century developed satellite communities which grew into towns in their own right. Several of them grew and nurtured such offshoots within their own original bounds. Others received extensions adjacent to their land. Still others planted villages on sites at a distance. Boston's subcolony of Braintree, and the satellites of Cambridge which became Billerica and Newton, may serve as representatives of this mode of growth.

Boston, capital, chief seaport and commercial center of the Massachusetts Bay colony, encountered early the problem of making a limited tract of land accommodate a growing population. There, of course, it soon became apparent that agriculture was not to be the leading occupation. By 1634 John Winthrop was arguing for a town policy of small allotments and a numerous population. " The reason " as he put it " why some were not willing that the people should have more land in the bay than they might be likely to use in some reasonable time, was partly to prevent the neglect of trades, and other

more necessary employments and partly that there might be
place to receive such as should come after; seeing it would
be very prejudicial to the commonwealth, if men should be
forced to go far off for land, while others had much, and
make no use of it, more than to please their eye with it." [1] In
a contested election, Winthrop won a place on a town board
of alloters, instructed to "devide and dispose" the town's
lands "to the inhabitants ... according to the Orders of the
Court, leaving such proportions in common for the use of
new Commers and further benefitt of the towne, as in theire
discretions they shall thinke fitt." [2]

Even a policy of encouragement of trades left some Bostonians with a desire and a need for land. For one thing, the
town could not for many years to come comfortably and con-
veniently bring in from elsewhere all the milk, fresh produce
and fodder for draft animals that it needed, and some hus-
bandry continued to be carried on both by part-time farmers
with other trades and by producers for the local market. For
another, there may well have been those who preferred or
were better equipped for farming, and we know that some
Bostonians seized the opportunities that arose to acquire
plowland and pasture elsewhere. To supplement the limited
area of its peninsula, Boston was permitted to lease Hog, Deer,
Long and Spectacle Islands [3] and was granted land at Pullen
Point and rights to cut wood on Dorchester neck. [4] The town
owned a tract at Muddy River (later Brookline) which the
colony offered to Thomas Hooker's company at Cambridge
as an inducement to stay in the Bay colony. Boston in return
was given "inlargement" at Mt. Wollaston and Rumney
Marsh. [5] When Hooker's people moved to Connecticut, Muddy

1 Winthrop *Journal*, p. 143.
2 Boston *Records*, p. 3.
3 Mass. *Records*, I, 115, 139.
4 Mass. *Records*, I, 101.
5 Mass. *Records*, I, 119, 129-130.

River reverted to Boston and both it and Mt. Wollaston were gradually divided among those of the town's inhabitants who had unsatisfied common rights.

Among the early grants by the town to individuals at Mt. Wollaston were several in 1635, 1636 and 1637 of fairly generous size to members of the so-called Antinomian party in Boston. John Wheelwright, William Hutchinson and William Coddington took up farms there.[6] Wheelwright preached to a congregation there, and Bostonians were in 1637 projecting a settlement to develop into a new town.[7] Some of the grantees of the Wheelwright congregation became permanent residents, but this particular project of plantation was set back by Wheelwright's and Mrs. Hutchinson's banishment and the departure of its leaders for Exeter and Rhode Island.

From 1637 to 1642 about 129 grants of tracts of moderate size were made by Boston.[8] Most of these were grants apparently to masters of families of 4a per head for the members of their households, though the record does not show whether servants were included or whether "estate" was represented by head-right equivalents. The number of heads per individual grant ranged from one to thirteen. In all, I count the names of 138 persons to whom Boston made Mt. Wollaston grants between 1634 and 1660. Of these, 110, as far as I can tell, resided very briefly or not at all in Braintree. Twenty eight are mentioned as inhabitants by the Braintree records, and 9 men apparently sons or relatives of these. For about 35 inhabitants I find no record of how they obtained their land. The obvious surmise is that they purchased from some of the 110 absentee owners. Most of the latter were

6 Boston *Records*, pp. 6, 7, 15.

7 Boston *Records*, p. 14. Committee "for the ripening thereof how there may bee a Towne and Church there." 10 Dec. 1636. C. F. Adams, in the second and third of his "Three Episodes of Massachusetts History" gives a thorough discussion of the Antinomians of Mt. Wollaston and of the general history of Braintree's development.

8 Boston *Records*, pp. 15-63.

Bostonians; most of the Braintree planters were apparently recent arrivals.

Until 1640 Mt. Wollaston was a part of the town of Boston. John Wheelwright had briefly preached there before his banishment. At the time of the Antinomian uproar his departure and that of several other of the grantees [9] deprived the church there not only of its minister but of other resources, and there was a churchless period of some years. In 1639 William Tompson and Henry Flint were called to the ministry of a church newly gathered in a covenant which they and six other men signed.[10] The following spring the settlement became the town of Braintree by two successive steps.

In an agreement between the town of Boston and " o͏ʳ neighbors of Mount Woollaston," the parent town transferred land titles and its own taxing power to the settlers, for a consideration and with reservations. Inhabitants of the new town were to pay " 4sh the acre for 2 acr of the 7 ac [11] formerly granted to divers m[en] of Boston upon expectation that they should have continued still with us, & 3 s the ac for euery acre wch hath bene or shalbee granted to any others who are not inhabitants of Boston." Certain tracts were turned over to the new town as common land, and 120a were donated to Tompson and 80a to Flint as a ministerial grant, but Boston reserved the power of disposing of all other common land, and of taxing privately owned tracts whose owners had not made the specified payments.[12] This contract thus called for a cash payment to cancel future tax obligations, reserved substantial amounts of land to Boston and to indi-

9 Samuel Allen, John Arnold, Wm. Balston, Wm. Coddington, Wm. Cole, Edward & Wm. Hutchinson, Nicholas Needham, Sampson Shatton, Wm. Wardall and perhaps Hugh Gunnison.

10 Pattee, *History of Braintree*, p. 194; Adams, *Three Episodes*, II, 586-7.

11 Adams takes this to mean 4s per acre for 2/7 of their acres. *Three Episodes*, II, 588.

12 Mass. *Records*, I, 291-292; Boston *Records*, p. 47.

vidual absentee owners and limited the new town's power
to tax the latter. The parties then petitioned the General
Court, which "granted them to bee a towne according to the
agreement with Boston," and named the new town Braintree.[13]

Braintree's contract of separation put her in something of
a unique position. The degree to which the new town's land
was mingled with land belonging (both title and jurisdiction)
to Boston, or to individual absentee owners, was greater than
in other cases. In 1647 Braintree compounded with Boston
for a cancellation of the older town's remaining tax privileges
there and purchased an additional 1500a of common land,
leaving ownership of the remaining unallotted land with Boston.[14] Edward Johnson commented at the time that "some
of Boston retain their farms from being of their Town, yet
do they lye within their bounds, and how it comes to pass I
know not."[15] Two and a half centuries later, a historian of
the town described Boston's reserved right in the new settlement as a proposal to "transplant the feudal system to America" and to gain for Boston an unearned increment appro-
priated from the efforts and improvements of Braintree
householders.[16]

Braintree's land commanded at the time of the separation
a fairly high relative market value and its owners saw no
reason to sell below their market. The frontier was receding,
and homesteads in established towns had already a substantial
market value. The settlers of Braintree acquired, close to the
high point of the wave of Puritan migration,[17] a part of the

13 Mass. *Records*, I, 291.

14 Braintree *Records*, pp. 14, 15.

15 Johnson, *Wonder Working Providence*, pp. 197-198.

16 Adams, *Three Episodes*, II, 651.

17 Since the agreement was reached by January 1640, and ratified the
following May, very likely its makers had no inkling of the political changes
in England which were shortly to reduce somewhat the incentives to emigrate.

limited remaining usable land near Massachusetts Bay. The church and the commoners of Boston obtained a fairly high price for property rights which had fallen to their share in the process of land distribution.

BILLERICA

Cambridge was the youngest of the original towns set about Boston Harbor. First named New Town, it was developed with assistance from the Colony government in 1631 and 1632, and became in 1633 the home of the Puritan ministers Thomas Hooker and Samuel Stone and their following. By 1636 Hooker and most of his church had concluded that the site on which they had planted was not large enough, had sold their lands and moved to Connecticut. A new church was gathered under Thomas Shepard's ministry, the town was named Cambridge and Harvard College established there. The subsequent growth of the town led to the settlement of two villages which grew from clusters of outlying grants to become independent towns.

One of these villages was on a site which first, so far as we know, attracted interest in 1636. In that and the following year the General Court directed that surveys be made of Shawshin, a tract lying north and west of Cambridge to determine whether it was " a fitt place for a plantacon."[18] A later surveying party in 1642 reported " that for the quantity it is sufficient, but for the quality in o^r app'hensions no way fit, the upland being very barren, & very little medow there about, nor any good timber almost fit for any use . . . the most p^t of all the good land is given out already: more land there is . . . but littell medow, & the upland of little worth. . ."[19]

Shawshin was, thus, available for settlement in the late 1630's, but not as promising a site as some others. In 1637 it had apparently been considered and rejected, in 1640 it was offered by the General Court to Cambridge and then to

18 Mass. *Records*, I, 1257, 2000.
19 Mass. *Records*, II, 10-11.

Roxbury with no result. In 1641 it was granted to Cambridge, " pvided the make it a village, to have 10 families there setled wthin three yeares ... ; " in 1642 the grant was repeated with a time limit of five years, and in 1644 these conditions were removed, the grant then having only the proviso that " the church & psent elders continue at Cambridge." [20]

Cambridge was deliberate enough in developing the land thus granted. In 1648 a town meeting reserved a " farme ... of a thousand acres, to be for a publick stock & improued for the Good of the Church, & that part of the Church that here shall Continue, & euery prson or prsons that shall from time to time remoue from the church: doe herby resigne up there intrest therein to the remaineing prt of the Church of Cambridge." [21] The town then offered " that those who doe, eyther resigne up there small farmes for the good of the towne, or doe want what they Can not be suplyed With in the bounds of the eight mile according to the nature of there grant ... should haue there prportions, for quantity & quality at Shawshine. allsoe there was then granted to seuerall brethren that had no house right in the town if they did desire it. farmes, at shaw shine." [22] Six individual grantees under these provisions were then named, and five townspeople appointed to " lay out to euery man there proportio."

The grantees under this town order may have occupied and used their land shortly after. A year later, three of them had the extent of their grants set at 500a apiece.[23] In 1650

20 Shawshin in Mass. *Records*, I, 167, 3 Mar. 1636 and I, 200, 1 Aug. 1637: committees to view; I, 306, 7 Oct. 1640: Cambridge to consider it for a village for one month, then Roxbury until the next General Court. I, 330, 2 June 1641: Grant to Cambridge, if ten families within three years. II, 17, 14 June 1642: Granted if village within five years. II, 62, 7 Mar. 1644: Granted with no condition of a village.

21 Cambridge *Records*, p. 74.

22 Cambridge *Records*, p. 75.

23 Cambridge *Records*, pp. 82, 83. Henry Dunster, President of Harvard college had a grant of 400a for himself and 100a for the college; Mr. Daniell Googin, Mr. Edward Collins " with some addition in respect of his place in the Deacon's office."

Thomas Danforth was given the year's "use and Improvement of the reserved Common meadow at shawshine," a grant repeated the following year with the marginal note "Town clerk his pay." [24] Early in 1651 the Church farm was offered for lease,[25] and was probably occupied by 1654 by John Parker.[26] These steps left substantial supplies of ungranted land.

In June 1652 the town undertook a general division of lands at Shawshin among its own commoners, it being "agreed that eurie man shall haue a proportion of the land more or lesse, according to his prportion now allotted him." The lots were to be laid out, after previous grants had been satisfied, "in two devisions between ye riuers and a 3d deuision on the east side shaw shin Riur and so euery mans lott to follow one another takeing all the 8 breadths at once the nearest land to the first Center being still alwaies the next lott in order." The names of 115 men were drawn and listed in order with the acreage to which each was entitled.[27]

Probably this division was never surveyed and laid out according to the town's order. Within the next few years a series of transactions had been completed which transferred much of the land to the new settlement and its planters. In 1652 Thomas Dudley sold a 1500 acre farm to three men of Woburn, who apparently conveyed it to the nine Woburn,

24 Cambridge *Records*, pp. 89, 93.

25 Cambridge *Records*, p. 94.

26 Hazen, *History of Billerica*, p. 24.

27 The total distribution was 10,870 acres. The 115 shares ranged from 10a to 450a; the arithmetic mean was 94½a. Approximately one half the individual grantees had 60a or less, one half had 80a or more. The most common size of individual grants was 80a (18), with 16 of 60a and 11 each of 50a and 20a.

The grants were distributed as follows:

6 of 10a	11 of 50a	7 of 100a	1 of 220a
6 of 15a	16 of 60a	2 of 140a	1 of 250a
11 of 20a	6 of 70a	5 of 150a	3 of 300a
3 of 30a	18 of 80a	1 of 180a	1 of 400a
5 of 40a	6 of 90a	4 of 200a	1 of 450a

Cambridge and Watertown planters who were resident there in 1654.[28] At about the same time the town of Cambridge apparently made a " township grant " of 400 acres, on which others settled.[29] In 1656 the General Court granted the plantation, which had then become a separate town named Billerica, 8000 acres " in any place or places that are ffree & not capeable of making a toune," [30] which was offered to the proprietors of the grants made by Cambridge in exchange for their titles. In a general deed, probably drawn up in 1659, all but 27 of the 115 grantees signed over their claims to the new town.[31]

Billerica's historian believes that the first permanent households in the Shawshin village were established in 1652 or 1653. He names nine families resident there in 1654.[32] In that year fourteen men signed a petition to the General Court asking for a new name, an independent town government and another patch of land just beyond their bounds along the Concord River. The following May the Court granted the land and the name, and confirmed the agreement between the villagers and a committee of the town of Cambridge by which the new community became an independent taxing and governing unit, " alwajes freed & acquitted from all manner of comon charges & rates, of what nature or kindesoeuer, due or belonging of right to be pajd vnto Cambridge by virtue of any graunt of that place vnto them by the Gennerall Court." [33] Cambridge stipulated that unimproved holdings by its own inhabitants were not to be taxed by Shawshin, but agreed that such holders should not be permitted to sell without the consent of the new town, and that their lands once

28 Hazen, *History of Billerica*, pp. 23, 26-28, 10-11.

29 Hazen, *History of Billerica*, p. 23.

30 Mass. *Records*, IV-I, 268-269.

31 Hazen, *History of Billerica*, p. 23.

32 Hazen, *History of Billerica*, p. 23.

33 Mass. *Records*, IV-I, 238-240.

transferred or improved "shall pay to the comon charges of . . . Shaushin . . . in due proporcon wth the rest of the inhabitants in that place." The municipal existence of Billerica dates from the ratification and approval of this agreement by the General Court.

The owners of what had been Dudley's 1500 acre farm had paid £110 for the tract, which was for convenience divided into twelve equal shares, each consisting of 113 acres of upland and 12 acres of meadow. Planters on the common land of Billerica, or on the lots purchased with the 8000 acres granted by the colony for that purpose, paid little or nothing as purchase price. The latter in 1658 agreed to assume one-half the purchase price of the Dudley land by a rate among themselves, a nominal "ten-acre lot" being the equivalent in land divisions and tax liabilities to a single share of the farm. The rate applied at that time came to not quite the promised £55, but it was probably collected from inhabitants admitted later, and there may have been an excess over the required sum.[34] If so, the excess may have been used to make the several purchases of land from private owners by which Billerica added subsequently to its supplies of common lands.[35] If the terms of the town's agreement with the Dudley purchasers were applied, inhabitants admitted to Billerica obtained 125 acres for 1/12 of £55, or not quite £4/10, payable in equal instalments one and two years after taking up the land.

Hazen mentions 43 Billerica inhabitants before 1660, of whom he traces 12 to previous homes in Cambridge, 7 to Woburn, 6 to Braintree and 2 to Watertown.[36] Samuel Whiting started preaching there in 1658, five years after his graduation from Harvard College.[37] In 1658 and 1659 the town

34 Hazen, *History of Billerica*, pp. 31-32, 54-55.

35 On p. 13 and 14 Hazen lists three purchases of land by Billerica from individual Cambridge grantees, totalling 770a.

36 Hazen, *History of Billerica*, 26-29.

37 Hazen, *History of Billerica*, 152-154.

made divisions of meadow and upland among its inhabitants, and in 1661 got an addition of 4000a from the General Court. Braintree and Billerica are samples of the towns planted by older towns on grants of new land by the colonial General Court. A number of other towns' villages on adjoining land grants grew into towns. Watertown in 1637 was granted the village which was to become Sudbury. Lynn Village was granted in 1639 and became the town of Reading in 1644. In 1640 Charlestown and Salem received tracts which became the towns of Woburn (1642) and Manchester (1645). Dedham's extension of 1649 became Medfield in 1651. Duxbury in Plymouth colony revieved a grant which grew between 1644 and 1656 to the town of Bridgewater, and Hartford and Windsor planted Farmington (a town in 1645) and Simsbury on their western borders. The outpost at West-field became an adjunct of Springfield in 1647, and later grew to a town. Villages at a distance were granted to Watertown (Dedham 1636), and to groups of inhabitants in Concord and Woburn (Chelmsford 1653), Ipswich (Brookfield 1660) and Braintree (Mendon 1660).

NEWTON

Cambridge's other village south of Charles River was developed gradually as part of the parent town on part of its original land.[38] Residents south of the river took their lands there as a part of the general division of lots in the town. In an enumeration of the holdings of 98 individual inhabitants of Cambridge in 1642, 40 are shown to have land south of the Charles River.[39] Eight of these south side holdings in-cluded dwelling houses, and probably at least two of these were regularly inhabited.[40] The town and land records of Cambridge give, with some gaps, an account of a series of

38 Mass. *Records*, I, 166, bounds to run 8 mi. from their meeting house.

39 Cambridge *Proprietors' Records*, pp. 72-116, "A Transcript of the houses and Landes of the Inhabitants of this Towne of Cambridge."

40 Smith, *History of Newton*, p. 40.

individual grants and divisions of land, and of sales and purchases whereby a number of Cambridge householders con-
centrated their holdings on one or the other side of the river.
In the years following 1634 the long, relatively narrow strip
of land included in modern times in the boundaries of
Brighton and Newton progressed from use as a common
pasture where the town's dry cattle were kept to a subordinate
community which by 1660 included about 15 families,[41] and
was prepared to take steps in the direction of independence
from the parent town.

Cambridge, which had apparently been willing enough to
encourage the separation of Billerica, resisted the attempts
at division on the part of the south side inhabitants. In 1635
the selectmen responded with a strong negative to the proposal that the remote households be free to call their own
minister.

> In answer to the request of some of or Beloved Brethren
> and Neighbours the Inhabitants on the south side of the River,
> that they might have the ordinances of Christ amongst them
> distinct from the Towne. The Townsemen not well vnder-
> standeing wt they intend, or do desire of the Towne, nor yet
> being able to conceive how any thing can be granted by the
> Towne in that respect, but ye fraccon will prove destructive to
> the whole body, Do not see ground to give any incouragement
> for any divissio of the Towne. Also wee hope that it is not the
> desire of or Bretheren so to accomoda[te] themselves by a
> division as thereby vtterly to dissinable and vndoe the Church
> of Christ with whome they have made so sollemn an ingage-
> ment in the Lord, wch is apparent to us wilbe the effect
> thereof and theref[ore] do desire that wee may Joyne both in
> hand & heart to worship the Lord together in one place vn-
> till the Lord shalbe pleased to inlarge & show vs or way more
> cleare for a divission.[42]

41 Smith, *History of Newton*, p. 40.
42 Cambridge *Records*, p. 107.

In this reply the town started to develop its plea that the proposed division would leave it too scantily supplied with resources to sustain itself properly, a plea which was to delay the completion of the process for many years.

The would-be seceders promptly appealed their case to the General Court, which appointed a committee of four men to investigate the case.[43] The committee was continued for two years, and reported in 1657 a recommendation against the petitioners.

> 1. Wee conceive that if the peticoners should wthdrawe
> theire help from theire contributing to Cambrdg church and
> ministry, it would be over burdensome to Cambridge to pro-
> vide for theire carrying an end those occasions; 1. Because it
> is acknowledged on both partjes the majnetenance at present
> is short enough, and our charitje leadeth vs to beleive they
> want not love either to theire minister or ministrje. 2. Because
> wee know some considerable persons haue removed on such
> groundes, and others seeme to intend it, tho indeered to the
> present ministrje amongst them, and many of them in an
> ebbing conditjon referring to outward things.
>
> 2. Referring to the brethren who haue petitioned freedome
> to be in a way of providing for theire supplye of a minister
> amongst them, who doe tender tenn pounds p anum towards
> Cambridge ministrje, tho wee acknowledge they are exposed
> to tempting difficultjes to moove, yett it seems not con-
> venient at the present to separate from theire brethren; 1. In
> regard of the feared incapacitje amongst themselves to errect
> theire desires; 2. In regard of some decljning as to the prose-
> cution of the worke amongst themselves; 3. Considering
> howgreivous it is to theire brethren, who professe much care
> & respect vnto them, which wee conceive may moove them
> still to wajte on the Lord, in the expectation of a further dis-
> couery of his minde heerein as referring to either partje. . .[44]

43 Mass. *Records*, IV-I, 228, 284, 291.

44 Mass. *Records*, IV-I, 319.

Perhaps the Lord discovered his mind to the south side people sufficiently to move them to call a preacher for winter service in 1659 and 1660, for Cambridge town meeting voted that winter that the "remote inhabitants" there "should annually be abated the one halfe of y^r prporccon to the ministryes allowance dureing the time they were prvided of an able minister according to law."[45] Before long the General Court conceded to the villagers that "all such lands & estate as are found to be more than fower miles from the meeting house, together with the persons thereon dwelling, shall be freed from contributing towards the ministry on the north side the riuer. . ."[46] John Eliot, Jr., Harvard College 1656, was ordained minister of the village's new church in 1664, and may have preached informally from 1657 or 1658 on.[47]

The village thus won leave to complete the ecclesiastical separation. In 1662 the laying out of eight divisions or "Squadrants" of land on the south side was recorded,[48] the commoners perhaps wishing to prepare for a civil separation. The latter, when it was achieved, set off the lands beyond the four-mile line as the town of Newton.[49] But the process took nearly thirty years more for completion, and evoked further pleas from Cambridge that the withdrawal would undermine its ability to support its church and its public responsibilities.

Similar divisions of other towns often took less time to complete. Plymouth and Duxbury reached an understanding in the years 1636-1638 which left the latter with its own local government. Outlying homesteads in Salem planted from 1639 on, became the town of Wenham in 1643, and

45 Cambridge *Records*, p. 130.

46 Mass. *Records*, IV-II, 16.

47 Smith, *History of Newton*, pp. 195-196.

48 Cambridge, *Proprietors' Records*, pp. 140-144.

49 Smith, *History of Newton*, pp. 72-77. Paige, *History of Cambridge*, pp. 79-96.

farms near the boundary between Ipswich and Salem were given the privilege of a separate minister in 1645 and made the town of Topsfield in 1648. Marblehead, another part of Salem's land, was set off in 1649, and Malden separated from Charlestown in the same year. About 1636 inhabitants of Dorchester were dwelling beyond the Neponset River in a village later to become the town of Milton.

CHAPTER V
RELIGIOUS DIVERSITY

THE Puritan colonists planned a structure of society in which recognizable religious truths would be accepted by the community in general. Few or none of them believed that it was safe to permit beliefs and opinions differing from the truth to be professed publicly. Where such differences did exist, they created not only a spiritual danger but many practical difficulties. Rifts in religious unity almost inevitably developed into disagreements about political and social problems.

Such differences were not readily avoidable in Puritan New England. The foundation of orthodoxy was a systematic program of learned interpretation and logical development of the principles of Christian ecclesiastical and social theory. But there were men of learning and apparent piety who arrived at varying conclusions, and there were laymen who challenged the system by professing to find a short cut to salvation without the intermediation of a learned ministry. The frontier served as an escape and refuge for those whose opinions became incompatible with those of their neighbors, and divergencies of opinion were the motive of several projects of plantation.

Roger Williams' personal idiosyncrasies of belief became intolerable to Massachusetts, and he was banished from the colony. But it was not difficult for him to purchase unclaimed land from the Indians, invite other planters to share in the venture and start the new town of Providence. When the Antinomian movement was at its height, Thomas Hooker's opposition to it may have encouraged him to push the project which was to remove his church to Connecticut. At the turn of the tide, many of the Antinomians themselves were forced or persuaded to withdraw from Massachusetts, and planted Portsmouth and Newport on Rhode Island and Exeter, New

Hampshire. The settlers of Warwick, R. I., irritated the Bay Puritans into actions which were both harsh and imprudent. A series of breaches troubled the Connecticut river towns in the first three decades of their history, resulting in several emigrations of dissident groups.

In the years 1635-1638 a debate of a philosophical issue of profound importance to the community of Puritans took place in Massachusetts. The party whose views ultimately became the official position dubbed its opponents Antinomians,[1] and contemporary and subsequent historians have written at length on the Antinomian controversy. The Antinomians developed a variant of Puritan religious theory which enjoyed a general popularity particularly in the Boston church, where one of the ordained ministers, John Cotton, preached a doctrine which seemed to support it. In the person of young Henry Vane, the party controlled for a year the Governorship of the colony, and when the General Court met in Boston it seems to have come under the influence of its host town's views.

In March of 1637 John Wheelwright was in Boston and had the not unusual experience of being asked, as a visiting minister, to address the church. He preached a sermon in which he reviewed and supported the charges of the Antinomians that the other ministers of the colony were preaching a covenant of works. By this he meant that they held that full compliance with the laws of church and state and outward acceptance of the duties of church membership were so clear an evidence of sanctification as to be effective proof of election. The General Court, notwithstanding Vane's ef-

1 The word Antinomian means against or opposed to law. Those who argued that salvation was a result of divine Grace and could not be earned by good behavior or observance of moral law undermined the philosophical foundation for the practice of using religion as a technique of law-enforcement. Their opponents then accused them of being contemners of all law and advocates of licentious behavior. As in the modern use of the similar word Anarchist, users of the term tended to infer that opposition to their own concepts of law and order tended to destroy legal institutions altogether.

forts as retiring governor to defend Wheelwright, held that this sermon was a denial of the validity of law which rendered its author guilty of contempt and sedition, and left to a later session the task of sentencing the convicted minister.[2] In May Vane failed of reelection, in August he returned to England and by the following November the Antinomians' influence in the General Court was approaching the vanishing point. In the session of 2 November, the Court disfranchised and banished Wheelwright under the earlier conviction and convicted Ann Hutchinson of "traduceing the mi[niste]rs and their ministery."[3] Mrs. Hutchinson had further expounded Antinomian views in informal discussions in her home in Boston, had been excommunicated by the church there, and had proved to the satisfaction of both church and court that she believed her actions to be governed by immediate revelations of the divine will. The same court held that a certain "remonstrance or petition" presented to the May session by defenders of Wheelwright was a seditious libel, unseated Boston's deputies William Aspinwall and John Oliver, banished Aspinwall and disfranchised four others for "justifying" it.[4] Reconvening on November 20, the Court decided that there was a danger that Wheelwright's and Hutchinson's supporters "may, vpon some revelation, make some suddaine irruption vpon those that differ from them in iudgment" and by name ordered some sixty of them to deliver to an appointed custodian all weapons in their possession.[5] The following March, the Court named seventeen men who had announced their intentions of leaving the colony, and ordered them to appear at its May session if they had not previously departed.[6]

Thus Wheelwright, Mrs. Hutchinson and Aspinwall were under sentence of banishment, a number of others had been

2 Mass. *Records*, I, 189.
3 Mass. *Records*, I, 207.
4 Mass. *Records*, I, 205-207.
5 Mass. *Records*, I, 211-212.
6 Mass. *Records*, I, 223.

subjected to legal penalties and several were under threat of further punishment. Of seventy-four persons against whom I find some record of action in these cases, the major portion avoided banishment by acknowledging their errors or lived on quietly until the furor died down. Thirty-three of them moved on to one or another of the heretical plantations. Wheelwright and four of the disarmed Antinomians went to Exeter where in 1639 they joined with twenty-nine others in a plantation covenant.[7] Four Salem men from among those summoned to the May court in 1638 if they were not gone by then joined Williams' plantation at Providence. The other twenty-four moved in the spring and summer of 1638 to Aquidneck or Rhode Island in Narragansett Bay. There the town of Portsmouth was built, a plantation covenant drafted and subscribed and deeds to the island secured from the Indians.

The first Portsmouth covenant was dated 7 March 1638 and had 19 signers.[8] During the remainder of that year new inhabitants were admitted, so that the records mention 42 men in the town, all but a few of whom were either admitted inhabitants, landowners or signers of the covenant. By the end of 1640 at least 37 more had made their appearance. This was rapid growth, and in 1639, 37 or 38 Portsmouth inhabitants withdrew to the other end of the island. Nine of them (including William Coddington, John Coggeshall and two other signers of the Portsmouth covenant of the previous year) drew up and signed a plantation covenant.[9] By the end of the year Newport was probably the more populous of the two towns. The remaining Portsmouth settlers drew up and signed a new covenant.[10]

7 Bell, *History of Exeter*, p. 15. N. H. Historical Society *Collections*, I, 147-149.

8 Rhode Island *Records*, I, 52.

9 Rhode Island *Records*, I, 87.

10 Rhode Island *Records*, I, 70. Portsmouth R. I. *Records*, I, 1.

Portsmouth and Newport managed their affairs much as other plantations did. From time to time they cooperated together and with Providence as a loose confederacy, and in 1647 became part of the colony of Rhode Island and Providence plantations under the charter secured by Roger Williams. Neither town supported an official church or professed to expect the magistrate to maintain orthodoxy, and consequently they and the whole colony were frequented by Baptists, Quakers and other sectarians less common in the orthodox colonies. Aside from this tendency (which seemed horrible enough in itself) the Rhode Islanders and the heretical plantations generally failed to plumb the depths of anarchy and disorder to the extent that their neighbors feared and expected. But not for many more years would the other New England colonies admit their right to be recognized as civilized communities.

The emigration to Connecticut was projected in 1634, initiated in 1635 and carried out in 1636. Among the mingled motives which led to this undertaking there appears some degree of dissatisfaction with the Antinomian tendencies appearing in the Bay colony. The religious differences between Massachusetts and Connecticut never led to an avowed breach. But we may take the settlement of Connecticut as another example of the town-planting tendency ensuing from theological differences. Connecticut's own churches offer further instances of minorities withdrawing to the frontier.

Between 1630 and 1636 the communities around Massachusetts Bay became a populous group of towns. The ministers of the churches there played an important role in the development of the ideas on which the colony based its political structure. John Cotton of Boston and Thomas Hooker of Newtown (later to become Cambridge), although fairly close acquaintances, differed somewhat over the questions of Antinomianism. Cotton preached what was in a sense a more extreme form of evangelical Protestantism than Hooker. He laid greater stress on the importance of grace and the distinction between the elect and the ordinary run of unregenerate humanity. Hooker's concept of the church was somewhat more latitudinarian in the sense that he was a little more willing to allow church membership to people of sound belief and righteous behavior without considering as closely the inward process of conversion. Here then the problem of the inward conversion and its outward signs again was in issue.

It was from Cotton's ministry that the Antinomian faction had sprung. Wheelwright was his associate, the Hutchinsons, Coddington, Coggeshall and Aspinwall members of his flock. It was when the controversy was at its height that differences between Cotton and the rest became apparent, and later students have speculated whether conviction or expediency led him to take a position on which he could maintain his status as an orthodox Massachusetts Puritan. Hooker had reason to be dissatisfied with Cotton's secure and influential position as Teacher of the Boston church.

Geographically neither Boston nor Cambridge could become self-sustaining agricultural producers. In contact with the principal harbor of the region, they were in the path of migration and their populations inevitably grew. When New England colonization was sufficiently advanced to support commercial functions Boston was the town in which they developed. Cambridge was planted on a residue of land left between Charlestown and Watertown north of the Charles River, with its territory on the other bank limited by Boston and Roxbury. The territory into which it expanded had the outline of an hourglass, with the town at its narrow waist.[11] This made tillage and cattle-keeping difficult for any but a small population, and gave rise to a series of complaints over the straitness of the town's bounds. With commercial and government activities centering in Boston, Hooker's congregation became articulately conscious of the limits of their field of economic opportunity.

11 Paige, *History of Cambridge*, p. 3.

So the congregation of Newtown felt the impact of both economic and religious incentives when they made their decision to move to the Connecticut Valley. They were joined in the move by a major part of the church members of Dorchester, and minorities from Watertown and Roxbury.

No serious religious motivation appears in the emigration from these three towns, although Dorchester's pastor and church organization went along with the removal.

Several hundred families left Massachusetts Bay in 1634-1636 to settle the four towns of the Connecticut Valley. In moving they left land and improvements which were purchased by some of the swarm of newcomers. They moved to a region in which the claims of others were easily quieted, and which was naturally well-endowed. Some of them abated the heat of religious controversy by a geographical separation from the proximity of their opponents. Religious diversity, though still to be troublesome to New Englanders, won a limited foothold as part of the tissue of civilized life as Connecticut and Massachusetts lived in comfortable political cooperation in spite of some doctrinal differences.

The success and progress of the Connecticut Valley settlements has attracted the attention of enthusiastic and capable historians.[12] The new colony weathered the Pequot war, boundary and traffic disputes between the colonies, the neglect of the Long Parliament and Cromwell and the suspicious attitude of the later Stuarts. They were soon feeding themselves and exporting furs, wood, grain and cattle. Before its first decade was over, the Connecticut colony was developing new plantations and towns.

The communities of Hartford and Windsor had churches with settled ministers before they arrived at their new sites. Springfield was fortunate enough to call a pastor soon after its settlement who succeeded in commanding the respect of his audience. Wethersfield had neither church nor minister

12 Adams, *Ancient Wethersfield*; Andrews, *River Towns of Connecticut*; Stiles, *Ancient Windsor*; Trumbull, *History of Connecticut*, among others.

at its first settlement. Richard Denton came from Watertown in 1638 [13] but was not formally ordained in the new town. In a dispute over church affairs, he and thirty-three others withdrew and took up a New Haven grant of the tract where they planted the town of Stamford.[14] Henry Smith preached to the congregation there from 1641 till his death in 1648 at the age of 60.[15] But his ministry was marred by land disputes and dissatisfaction expressed by townspeople.[16] Then John Russell (Harvard 1645) was called to succeed Smith in 1649.[17] He subsequently became involved in the controversy over the Halfway Covenant, in which he maintained a strict doctrine and led a minority of the town in a withdrawal from the errors his opponents were maintaining throughout the colony.

In Hartford, Thomas Hooker ministered to the church he had joined in Newtown in 1633, and with which he had migrated, until his death in 1647. Samuel Stone, his fellow-alumnus of Emmanuel College, Cambridge and his long-time colleague, carried on in his place until 1663. John Warham had been from its founding a minister of the church which the settlers of Dorchester had gathered before sailing from England, and held his post through two migrations and 33 years of Windsor's history.[18] These men, aided by the prestige and the understanding acquired by long association with their congregations, kept their churches intact in the face of the strains which twice rent asunder that of Wethersfield. But the strains were there, and dissenters from both congregations joined in the withdrawal which planted the town of Hadley further up the river.

13 *Ancient Wethersfield*, p. 136; Conn. *Records*, I, 63; Morison, *Founding of Harvard College*, p. 378.

14 *Ancient Wethersfield*, p. 136.

15 Morison, *Founding of Harvard College*, p. 401.

16 Conn. *Records*, I, 44, 86, 97.

17 *Ancient Wethersfield*, p. 158.

18 *Ancient Windsor*, 19-23.

Puritan churches had the delicate and difficult duty of maintaining themselves as institutional oases of Saints amid a wilderness of original sin. A large proportion of mankind might have God's Grace working within them without any sure symptom by which they or others might tell it. What was to be the attitude of the church toward those who had not proven themselves regenerate by confession and repentance and who were therefore not full members? Wethersfield experienced a long wrangle in which the church and the town were arrayed against each other. First Richard Denton in 1640 and later John Russell in 1659 led their church organizations away from the town. The second withdrawal was joined by a minority of the Hartford church. Samuel Stone in Hartford and John Warham in Windsor were moving toward a broadening of the privileges of non-members.[19] The practice of " owning the covenant " was beginning. This was a device whereby the baptised sons and daughters of church members who were not themselves in full communion were permitted, after a simple assertion of their belief in Christian principles and obedience to the church, to present their own children for baptism. This " Halfway Covenant " was unacceptable to the pastor and most of the membership of the Wethersfield church, and to a minority of Hartford members.

In 1653 and 1654 a company of planters from Hartford and Windsor had obtained and settled on a grant of Massachusetts land north of Springfield, naming their town Northampton. Probably their removal had no particular connection with the religious controversy which was starting at about that time. But the land they acquired was one-half of a tract called Nonotuck which a committee of the Massachusetts General Court divided into two " plantations," reserving the other.[20] Thus it is not surprising that the Hartford and

19 Judd, *History of Hadley*, pp. 11-18; *Ancient Wethersfield*, pp. 160-161.
20 Mass. *Records*, IV-I, 136, 213.

Wethersfield "strict congregationalists" should think of the remaining site when they planned their removal. In a petition to the Massachusetts colony, the Hartford minority "conceive that it may be most for the comfort of them and theirs to remove themselves and families from thence, and to come under your pious and godly government. . ." and request "your gracious allowance to dispose ourselves" at Nonotuck.[21] The General Court agreed in 1658 to grant their request, "provided they submitt themselves to a due & orderly hearing of the differences betweene themselves & the rest of theire brethren."[22] This they did before a council of fourteen visiting ministers[23] and the Court the following year, observing "that there are many desirable psons hauing a pastor wth his church engaged to goe along wth them" granted the land and appointed a committee to lay out its bounds.[24] During the mild seasons of 1659, Russell and the former Wethersfield church, with about 29 men from Wethersfield and Hartford, settled in what shortly became the town of Hadley.

Religious dissent remained common enough as a secondary theme in American frontier movements. But Hadley was perhaps the last manifestation of the feeling that a group *must* move because of a religious difference of opinion. In Windsor the age and infirmity of John Warham brought the issue of the Half-way Covenant to a head a scant decade later. The solution adopted by the town and approved by the General Court permitted the majority to call a new minister and the minority to employ a "lecturer" who was permitted to preach to his party at stated times. When attempts at reconciliation failed, the dissidents were permitted to form their own society.[25] Boston already had its second church, and Hart-

21 Judd, *History of Hadley*, pp. 18, 19.
22 Mass. *Records*, IV-I, 328.
23 Judd, *History of Hadley*, p. 16.
24 Mass. *Records*, IV-I, 368.
25 Conn. *Records*, II, 124.

ford was soon to gather one. The Restoration government imposed a limited degree of toleration upon the colonies. At least, it was thenceforth possible for Christians to disagree and churches to split without necessarily driving people into exile or to the frontier.

CHAPTER VI

ACCOMMODATION OF NEWCOMERS

As the Puritan stream continued, each newly-arrived colonist was confronted with the problem of choosing a place to live. The range of choice available spread *pari passu* with the growth of geographical knowledge about the region. Many of the new colonists simply moved into towns already settled, or joined with companies they found in New England who were projecting new plantations. But a substantial number of ministers arrived during the 1630's, and they were commonly the leaders of groups who arrived with the intention of planting a town and gathering a church which would continue their former association. Several such pastors and their flocks, arriving between 1636 and 1640, selected new sites for plantations after their arrival in the Bay colony.

New Haven

On 26 June 1637 the *Hector* disembarked such a group of thirty-nine men from London, a number of them with families.[1] Their minister, John Davenport, had been vicar of St. Stephens, Coleman Street, where several of them had been his parishioners. An active Puritan, he had embraced a prudent exile in Holland from 1633 to 1635. He had been interested in the Virginia and Massachusetts Bay companies.[2] Theophilus Eaton, a prosperous merchant, was the leading layman of the company. These new colonists spent nine months as temporary residents of Charlestown, Roxbury and other towns before committing themselves to a choice of a plantation site. Eaton made at least one extended journey toward the tract finally chosen at Quinnipiack.[3] Davenport

1 Calder, *The New Haven Colony,* pp. 29-30, lists the passengers. Winthrop *Journal,* I, 223; Atwater, *History of the Colony of New Haven,* p. 58; Banks, *Planters of the Commonwealth,* p. 181.

2 Calder, *The New Haven Colony,* chapter I.

3 Winthrop *Journal,* I, 231.

spent the winter doing his share in the attempt to save Ann
Hutchinson from her errors and participating in the Antinomian controversy.[4]

What the company were looking for was a site where they
could establish a commercial town. They considered land in
various places and rejected "many offers here [in Massachu-
setts] and at Plymouth."[5] "Charlestown offered them
largely, Newbury their whole town, the court any place which
was free," but they finally chose the mouth of the Quinnipiack river as the site where they would plant the town of
New Haven and re-embarked for their removal in the spring
of 1638.[6] Two bachelors and one family head had left the
original group, but thirty-two men from various Massachusetts towns joined them.[7] The choice was the result of a
deliberate plan for the development of new commercial and
colonizing efforts, and a systematic search for a site where
the plan could be carried out.[8]

NEW HAVEN'S SATELLITES

New Haven was planted on land which belonged to nobody
but the Indians. The aboriginal titles were extinguished by
deeds of purchase signed late in 1638.[9] The town took to
itself the powers of local government in a "fundamental
agreement" on 4 June 1639,[10] limiting franchise to church

4 Winthrop *Journal*, I, 230, 235.

5 Winthrop *Journal*, I, 231.

6 Winthrop *Journal*, I, 265.

7 Calder, *The New Haven Colony*, 47.

8 To the present writer Newbury would appear to be the best of the sites
named as being under consideration. At the mouth of the Merrimac, it stood
to gain by the transshipment of the produce of the upriver towns, who were
on the threshold of a period of growth. But it may have seemed so near
Boston as to be destined for a subsidiary position. In any event, hindsight
is cheaper than foresight.

9 New Haven *Records*, I, 1-7.

10 New Haven *Records*, I, 10-17.

members, setting forth that ". . . the Scriptures doe holde forth a perfect rule . . . as well in the gou^rm^t of famylyes and comonwealths as in matters of the chur.", and nowhere mentioning the English Crown or acknowledging the nationality of the settlement. For a quarter-century this independent jurisdiction, without recognition from any European power, operated in the void between the vague boundaries of Connecticut and New Amsterdam.

This void soon attracted other plantations, some under New Haven's aegis and others adhering to the Connecticut colony. Peter Prudden, a Hertfordshire minister, was the leader of a group of 15 families who were fellow-travelers to New England with Davenport and Eaton.[11] In the summer of 1639 this group was occupying land in New Haven, and gathered their own church there, independent of Davenport's church.[12] That fall they negotiated with New Haven for the sale of their lots to the town,[13] and Prudden's church, with a total of 19 planters, moved a few miles west to develop the town of Milford. Others from Wethersfield and elsewhere increased the initial population of the town to 54 men.[14] The plantation governed itself independently until in 1634 it entered a " consociation " with New Haven, sending deputies to the General Court there and submitting to its jurisdiction over the federated towns.[15]

Southold, on Long Island, and Guilford became the homes of similar minister-led groups which came out from England after the New Haven company. Southold's site was bought by New Haven and granted to John Younge and his associates as a plantation under the older community's colonial jurisdiction.[16] In 1639 about 25 men newly come from Eng-

11 Calder, *The New Haven Colony*, p. 47.

12 Atwater, *History of the Colony of New Haven*, p. 155.

13 New Haven *Records*, I, 24.

14 Atwater, *loc. cit.*, *Ancient Wethersfield*, p. 134.

15 New Haven *Records*, I, 110-111.

16 New Haven *Records*, I, 70, 463; Atwater, *op. cit.*, pp. 171, 172.

land under Henry Whitfield's ministry covenanted to form a town and purchase land at Menunkatuck.[17] By 1643 their town, then named Guilford, was also a member of the New Haven jurisdiction.[18] Both Stamford and Branford, plantations projected and governed by the New Haven colonial government, were occupied by emigrants from Wethersfield.[19]

Although lacking charter or grant, the New Haven colonial jurisdiction was accepted as an equal by the other Puritan colonies. It was a member of the United Colonies and had its Governor, General Court and machinery of colonial and local administration on the usual Puritan pattern. After 1660 it failed to apply for a charter to the Restoration government, and was absorbed into Connecticut under that colony's new charter.

Rowley

Ezekiel Rogers was another Puritan minister of some note who led a group to New England in 1638. Originally he intended to join Davenport and Eaton in the New Haven colony, and some of his companions were there temporarily in 1638 or 1639.[20] But he was dissatisfied with the accommodations offered there, and more strongly attracted to a site between Ipswich and Newbury. There his company bought some outlying farms from Ipswich owners,[21] and " had granted them 8 miles every way into the countrey, where it may not trench vpon other plantations already setled." [22] Winthrop noted that on Rogers' arrival he had with him " some

17 Atwater, *op. cit.*, p. 160.

18 New Haven *Records*, pp. 96, 199.

19 Atwater, *History of the Colony of New Haven*, p. 174, 595-598; Adams, *Ancient Wethersfield*, p. 134 sqq.; New Haven *Records*, I, 47, 199-200.

20 Winthrop *Journal*, I, 297-298.

21 Winthrop *Journal*, I, 298.

22 Mass. *Records*, I, 253.

twenty families," [23] but by 1643 59 lots had been distributed in Rowley among individual owners.[24] In several cases more than one member of a family had a lot, but it seems certain that the group had grown larger since Rogers' arrival.

New Haven, Milford, Guilford, Southhold and Rowley were all settled by ministers and men who wanted to be members of their congregations. Most of the many Puritan ministers who arrived in New England between 1630 and 1640 brought with them or attracted admirers and adherents. Some, like John Cotton, Nathaniel Ward and John Eliot, were called to church office in towns already settled. Others moved from town to town with their followers. Stephen Batchelor settled at Lynn, where he presently was accused of irregular church proceedings. He thereupon led his small flock to Yarmouth on Cape Cod, and thence moved to Hampton.[25] Finally at an advanced age he returned to England. Richard Blinman and his group stayed briefly in Marshfield and lived in Gloucester from 1641 to 1648. John Winthrop, Jr., induced them to populate his projected plantation of New London in 1650. Blinman also finally left New England, going to Newfoundland in 1659 and thence to England. Nathaniel Ward's son, John, a minister and a graduate of Cambridge, lived briefly with his father in Ipswich, and then, with Giles Firmin and others, obtained a grant of land and planted the town of Haverhill.[26]

These ministers were leaders in the planting of their towns. They served as organizing forces to bring together the number of planters required to start a town. They sometimes took an active part in the choice of a site. To some extent every

23 Winthrop *Journal*, I, 298.

24 Quotation from Rowley Town Records in Gage, *History of Rowley*, pp. 123-129.

25 Winthrop *Journal*, I, 162, 266.

26 Mather, *Magnalia Christi Americana*; Morison, *Founding of Harvard College* and Weis, *The Colonial Churches and The Colonial Clergy of New England* contain compilations of information concerning these and other ministers of the period.

new minister who arrived made the planting of a new town possible,[27] and every project for a new town opened an opportunity for a new minister. In the 1640's Harvard College began graduating annual classes of young men who supplied vacancies after the decline in immigration and the almost complete drying up of the supply of English ministers in that decade.

27 But some towns had two, and a few had three ministers at a time.

CHAPTER VII
SOME PURITAN PROMOTERS

PURITAN colonization offered a field of opportunity to a number of individuals who used more-than-ordinary talents of imaginative ambition, specialized knowledge and access to capital and credit to attain personal success. Such men made considerable contributions of planning and managing services, conducted a wide variety of mercantile operations and enjoyed a standard of material wealth and comfort which placed them above the ordinary run of their neighbors in this respect. They were sufficiently like the successful and innovating business man of the latter-day capitalist economy to make the comparison useful. At the same time, they fitted into the Puritan scheme as useful and honorable instruments of the plan for building a civilized and Christian community.

John Winthrop, Jr., son of Governor Winthrop, had an important hand in the development of four towns in three of the Puritan colonies. He projected ironworks and organized a company of English investors which sent funds and workers to initiate them. He was a prospector for mineral deposits, a naturalist and medical practitioner, a grower of livestock and a magistrate. He and his family dwelt successively in Boston, Ipswich, Saybrook and New London.

Winthrop arrived in New England first in November of 1631,[1] with his stepmother and his wife. He rejoined his father's household for the time being, and became an Assistant the following May.[2] Just over a year after his arrival, he received from the Assistants a mandate to lead one of the earliest groups of settled New Englanders to plant a new town. The Governor describes his alarm at the rumor of a French colonial venture at Cape Sable, and his consultation with the Assistants, ministers and captains, who agreed on

1 Winthrop *Journal*, I, 70.

2 Winthrop *Journal*, I, 79.

the need to fortify the approaches to Boston Harbor. They also decided that a " plantation should be begun at Agawam, (being the best place in the land for tillage and cattle,) least an enemy, finding it void, should possess and take it from us. The governor's son (being one of the Assistants) was to undertake this, and take no more out of the bay than twelve men; the rest to be supplied at the coming of the next ships." [3] Winthrop and his party broke ground in the new plantation in March 1633, and were building during the open season that followed.[4] The General Court in April accepted the plantation as a *fait accompli,* but asserted its right to control the admission of new inhabitants there. Eleven men including Winthrop were given leave to plant in the new town.[5]

The same spring Winthrop paid a visit to William Leveridge, minister at the Piscataqua settlement [6] and before long was broaching the subject of a call to him from the new town.[7] That fall Winthrop's house in Ipswich was nearing completion. His wife, waiting in Boston, was fearful of the prospect of a frontier winter, writing " prethee love make hast home," [8] but apparently some time between October 1633 and March 1634 had moved to the new house.[9]

In 1634 the new town received its English name [10] and an

3 Winthrop *Journal*, I, 97-98. That "the best place in the land for tillage and cattle" should thus be entrusted to the Governor's son and his associates did not, so far as I know, evoke the kind of suspicion that appears in similar incidents in more modern times.

4 Winthrop *Journal*, I, 99; *Winthrop papers*, III, 119, 120-121, 141-142.

5 Mass. *Records*, I, 103, 105; Winthrop *Journal*, I, 99, makes the total 13.

6 *Winthrop papers*, III, 120-121.

7 *Winthrop papers*, III, 140. The Governor wrote his son 24 October 1633, doubting that Leveridge was free to leave the post he then held, or that young Winthrop and his neighbors would be able to maintain him before the following spring.

8 *Winthrop papers*, III, 141, 142.

9 *Winthrop papers*, III, 146.

10 Mass. *Records*, I, 123. "It is ordered, that Aggawam shalbe called Ipswitch."

accretion of manpower in the arrival of Thomas Parker, " a
minister and a company with him, being about one hundred,
[who] went to sit down at Agawam. . ." [11] A year later
Parker moved on to Newbury. Ipswich was not long without
a minister, but Winthrop's attention was by that time elsewhere engaged. He had gone to England in the summer of
1634 [12] and returned in October 1635 " with commission from
Lord Say, Lord Brook, and divers other great personages in
England, to begin a plantation at Connecticut. . ." [13] Thereafter he returned only briefly to Ipswich. Nathaniel Ward,
Parker's successor in the pulpit there, wrote in 1635 of his
satisfaction with the town, adding " your absence hath bredd
us much sorrowe. . ." [14] and in 1637 the people of Ipswich
were petitioning the General Court not to give him duties
that would still keep him away.[15] But after 1634 Winthrop
lived only briefly (1637-1638) in the town.

His brief residence apparently qualified Winthrop for the
grant of two town lots of moderate size and two generous
farms. Argilla farm, apparently granted in 1634 with 320
acres of land, Winthrop sold to his kinsman Samuel Symonds
in the winter of 1637-1638.[16] Almost simultaneously he received from the town the grant of Castle Hill, including 100
acres of meadow and probably as much or more of upland.[17]
This land he held until 1645, but probably never had a dwelling
house there.[18] This allowance of land was fairly large, but

11 Winthrop *Journal*, I, 125-126.

12 He was in Aggawam in July, and in London in November. *Winthrop
papers*, III, 170, 175.

13 *Winthrop papers*, III, 198-199; Winthrop *Journal*, I, 161.

14 *Winthrop papers*, III, 215-217.

15 *Winthrop papers*, III, 432-433.

16 Waters, *Ipswich*, I, 517-518, 511; *Winthrop papers*, III, 518; IV, 11.

17 Waters, *Ipswich*, p. 516; Waters, *Winthrop*, p. 23; *Winthrop papers*,
IV, 4-5.

18 Waters, *Ipswich, loc. cit.*; Waters, *Winthrop*, p. 11.

several other inhabitants of Ipswich received allotments total-
ing 100 to 200 acres or more,[19] and his holdings were about
what one would expect for a man in his position.

Returning from England in 1635, Winthrop promptly took
up the Saybrook project. In November he sent an advance
party to " begin some building," and Lion Gardiner, " an ex-
pert engineer " sent by the lords and gentlemen, reported to
him in Boston.[20] Saybrook was for a number of years maintained in the interest of its English Puritan backers. Winthrop
was there in the spring of 1636, and kept up a correspondence
with the English owners about their affairs in the Connecticut
Valley.[21] That summer George Fenwick came to the outpost
as agent for the owners,[22] and Winthrop, though he continued
to take an interest in the region, returned to Ipswich at the
expiration of his one year's commission.[23] For the next few
years he was in Ipswich, Salem and Boston. He was an Assistant of the Massachusetts Bay Colony, a projector of salt
works at Salem [24] and an advisor to the settlers of Hampton
and Rowley.[25]

In 1640 Winthrop returned to England with a party of
ministers who were dispatched on receipt of the news of the
" general reformation " in hand there " to be ready to make
use of any opportunity God should offer for the good of the
country here, as also to give any advice, as it should be required, for the settling the right form of church discipline
there." [26] In England Winthrop, with Robert Bridges of

19 See the apparently incomplete reprinting of Ipswich land grants in
Essex county Historical and Genealogical Register, I, 163-164, 184-185;
II, 11-12, 37-39, 59.

20 Winthrop *Journal*, I, 165-166.

21 *Winthrop papers*, III, 198-319, *passim*.

22 *Winthrop papers*, III, 262.

23 Waters, *Winthrop*, p. 18.

24 *Winthrop papers*, III, 140-141.

25 *Winthrop papers*, III, 69-70, 139.

26 Winthrop *Journal*, II, 31, 32.

Lynn, improved his opportunities by raising £1000 from eleven " undertakers " to invest in an Ironworks in the colony.[27] Returning to Massachusetts, Winthrop successfully applied in 1644 and 1645 to the General Court for a monopoly and grants of land and wood, and projected works at Lynn and Braintree.[28] In 1645 Richard Leader was sent over by the undertakers to relieve Winthrop and operate the enterprise.[29]

Two projected mineral enterprises which never attained permanent success attracted Winthrop's attention to the Pequot country, where he carried out his next project of plantation. In a petition for a grant there in 1644 he reports iron ore deposits and states his intention of developing them.[30] But he was probably even more in earnest in his desire to develop the graphite or black lead mines near the headwaters of the Pequot River.[31] Armed with a Massachusetts colony grant [32] he apparently had Stephen Day at work on the spot in 1644, and contracted with Thomas King for a crew of miners to go up.[33] But transportation difficulties prevented successful development.[34]

Winthrop was already the owner, by both Massachusetts and Connecticut grants, of Fisher's Island off the coast of this region.[35] In 1644 the Massachusetts General Court gave him " liberty to make a plantation in the said Pequot country

27 Lewis and Newhall, *History of Lynn, 1629-1864*, p. 205; *Winthrop papers*, IV, 371-372.

28 Mass. *Records*, II, 61-62, 81-82, 103-104, 125-128. *Winthrop Papers*, IV, 422, 425-427.

29 *Winthrop papers*, V, 6-7, 27.

30 *Winthrop papers*, IV, 465-466; Mass. *Records*, II, 71.

31 I. e. the Thames River of later days.

32 Mass. *Records*, II, 82.

33 *Winthrop papers*, IV, 495, 497-498.

34 American Antiquarian Society *Proceedings*, second series, XIV, 471-497.

35 Mass. *Records*, I, 304; Conn. *Records*, I, 64-65.

wth such othero a3 shall psent themselves to ioyne in the said plantation." [36] In November 1645 he made a journey of exploration from Boston overland to Springfield, Hartford and Saybrook; thence along the coast eastward through the country where his grant lay "querendo loco commodo pro colonia" [37] and back through Rhode Island to the Bay.

Winthrop and his associates established themselves at the new plantation in 1646.[38] Thomas Peters was minister to the group for its first year, then left to return to England. These two were commissioned to govern the new settlement and treat with the Indians there.[39] In 1647 thirty-six house lots were laid out.[40] The right of the Massachusetts Bay colony to govern the area was questioned by Connecticut in 1646 before the Commissioners of the United Colonies.[41] Connecticut made good its claim and in 1649 granted the plantation three years exemption from public rates and appointed Winthrop and two assistants to hear small causes there.[42] In 1650 Richard Blinman [43] came from Gloucester to serve as pastor of the new church and brought about 20 families with him.[44]

Once Pequot (which became New London in 1658) was a thriving town, Winthrop began to find inducements to move elsewhere. George Baxter and William Hallett, having gone to live among the Dutch at Manhattan, wrote in 1649 with glowing offers of land on Long Island and influence with the Dutch government.[45] Edward Elmer of New Haven of-

36 Mass. *Records*, II, 71.

37 *Winthrop papers*, V, 51-54.

38 Caulkins, *History of New London*, p. 47; Winthrop *Journal*, II, 275.

39 Mass. *Records*, II, 160-161.

40 Caulkins, *History of New London*, pp. 47-70.

41 *Acts of the United Colonies*, I, 19, 79, 96-97.

42 Conn. *Records*, I, 185-186.

43 *Winthrop papers*, V, 148-150, 168, 189-190, 269-270, 272.

44 Caulkins, *History of New London*, pp. 66-69.

45 *Winthrop papers*, V, 355.

fered men and capital if Winthrop would undertake a plantation at Delaware Bay.[46] In the late 1650's he moved to New
Haven and thence to Hartford, where he was for several
terms governor of Connecticut and was the colony's agent in
London to obtain the charter of 1662.

The scope and success of Winthrop's promotion of enterprises and plantations seems to have been based on a number
of things. His elevation to political responsibility as Assistant
and as leader of the Aggawam plantation were things probably more likely to happen to a Governor's son than to others,
and his success in raising capital for his ironworks was somewhat the success of the Winthrop name. A reading of letters
to him from neighbors and business associates leaves the impression that he was a man of wide knowledge and ready
with advice and encouragement. His travels and his repeated
shifts of attention from old to new enterprises indicate an
exceptional vigor of body and mind. He was working in a
region where his active curiosity could not help seeing new
possibilities; he was so situated that colonial courts and towns
would give him land, political power and commercial monopo-
lies; individuals were willing to adventure their persons and
purses under his direction and he blended these factors into
an active and successful career.

THE PYNCHONS

William Pynchon came to Dorchester in 1630, and soon
moved to Roxbury. Son of an English country squire, he had
the position and means to become a man of position and influence.[47] So far as I can tell, it was taste and opportunity
rather than training that led him to establish a trading business and to purchase from the colony for £25 the beaver
monopoly at Roxbury.[48] Fur trade seemed attractive enough

46 *Winthrop papers*, V, 357-358, 361.

47 DAB; Morison, " William Pynchon, the Founder of Springfield" in
Proceedings of the Mass. Historical Society, LXIV (1932), p. 67 sqq.

48 Mass. *Records*, I, 100 (1632).

to him so that when the Connecticut Valley was settled he moved to establish himself on the new path of commerce. In 1636 he, with a number of fellow-planters from Roxbury and other New England towns, was building a trading-post and town upstream from all potential competitors.[49]

At first their new plantation of Agawam [50] was part of the confederation of river towns which became the Connecticut colony. Pynchon was a member of the commission of the government appointed by the Bay colony [51] and later a participant in the Connecticut General Court.[52] In the winter of 1637-1638 high food prices in Connecticut, the aftermath of the Pequot War, led the General Court there to appoint Pynchon as exclusive buyer of corn among the Indians of the upper valley. His markup was limited and competing buyers were restrained from bidding up prices against him.[53] The whole project seemed designed to make the most of the new plantations' weak bargaining position. But Pynchon failed to give satisfaction to his downstream neighbors, his monopoly was overset [54] and he was fined and widely criticized for taking improper advantage of his position.[55] It is

49 Of thirty-two landowners in the Springfield *Records* before 1640, Pynchon and two or four others came from Roxbury, six were from other Massachusetts towns. The remainder leave no record I have found of earlier New England residence. The early Roxbury town records are missing and they may have been from Roxbury. Roxbury *Records*, iii-v, *History of Roxbury*, pp. 6-7.

50 Later Springfield. The name Agawam was earlier applied to Ipswich (*vide supra*, p. 94) and later to a town across the river from Springfield.

51 Mass. *Records*, I, 170-171.

52 Conn. *Records*, I, 13, 17.

53 Conn. *Records*, I, 13.

54 Conn. *Records*, I, 14.

55 Conn. *Records*, I, 19. Green, *Springfield*, pp. 20-38. Baldwin, " The Secession of Springfield from Connecticut " *in Publications of the Colonial Society of Massachusetts*, XII (1911), p. 65. Morison, " William Pynchon, the Founder of Springfield " in *Proceedings of the Massachusetts Historical Society*, LXIV (1932), pp. 83-87. Morison's contention is that Connecticut wanted to impose a paternalistic trade regulation based on the concept of

perhaps not surprising in view of this contretemps that
Pynchon and his fellow-townspeople forthwith discovered
that they were "by godes provedence fallen into the line of
the Massachusete Jurisdiction" and tacitly severed the
political bonds which tied them to their Connecticut neighbors.[56] This transfer of allegiance was regarded downriver
as an act of duplicity. Thomas Hooker retorted:

> If Mr. Pynchon can devise ways to make his oath bind him
> when he will and loosen him when he list; if he can tell how,
> in faithfulness to engage himself in a civil covenant and com-
> bination (for that he did, by his committees in their act) and
> yet can cast it away at his pleasure, before he give it suffi-
> cient warrant, more than his own word and will, he must find
> a law in Agaam for it; for it is written in no law or gospel
> that ever I heard.[57]

Wherever he found the law for it this change had its advantages for Pynchon. Ninety nearly trackless miles separated
him from the seat of a General Court which gave him trading rights and executive and judicial power [58] and his path
to the sea lay through a jurisdiction which now must treat
him as a resident of a friendly but powerful neighboring colony rather than as one of their own. He successfully challenged Edward Hopkins' title to a trading post at Woronoco
and established a branch of his own enterprise there.[59] When
Connecticut imposed an export duty on goods shipped out of
the river at Saybrook, he and the Massachusetts colony went

just price, while Pynchon wanted to maintain a free market. But one can
just as well interpret Pynchon as a monopsonistic "bulk-buying" agent
of the Connecticut government's plan to restrain post-war inflation and his
rivals as individuals who wanted to insure their own supplies even if it
meant bidding up the price.

56 Morison, *op. cit.*, p. 88; *Winthrop papers*, IV, 98-99; Green, *Springfield*,
p. 60; *Acts of the United Colonies*, I, 21.

57 Green, *Springfield*, p. 43.

58 Mass. *Records*, I, 321; II, 44, 224.

59 Woronoco later became Westfield, Mass. Green, *Springfield*, p. 60;
Acts of the United Colonies, I, 21.

down to defeat in attempting to get it removed through the
United Colonies, but a retaliatory levy on intercolonial trade
entering Boston soon forced the removal of the offending
tax.[60]

Pynchon developed a successful trading business, shipping
corn and fur down the river and bringing up wampum and
trade goods. As a merchant and magistrate he traveled back
and forth to Boston both by land and by sea. A cart road
to Warehouse Point below the falls of the Connecticut at
Enfield was his contact with navigable water.[61] In the allotments of land at Springfield he received the largest individual
shares, a recapitulation in 1646 crediting him with 237
acres, two of his sons-in-law with 148 and 125 respectively
and no other individual with over 67.[62]

To commerce and politics Pynchon added theological
speculation as a field of endeavor. A tract of his authorship
printed in London entitled " The Meritorious Price of Man's
Redemption " reached New England in 1650. The Massachusetts General Court in its October term found the book heretical and ordered it burned on Boston Common.[63] Pynchon
was summoned before the Court and given a year to prepare
an answer.[64] But he decided to retire both from the controversy and from business and turned over his property in
Springfield to his son John and his sons-in-law Elizur

60 *Acts of the United Colonies*, I, 80, 89-93, 120-136, 155-156; Mass.
Records, II, 182-183, 269-270; IV-I, 11; Conn. *Records*, I, 119-120, 161,
189-190.

61 The boundary between Massachusetts and Connecticut, following for
the most part the charter line, now lies north of Enfield. But Massachusetts
surveyors, whose loyalty surpassed their accuracy, set it several miles farther
south. *Cf.* Mass. *Records*, II, 227, 264.

62 Springfield *Records*, I, 157, 158, 159, 163, 171, 172, 179, 190. These
figures apparently do not include undivided common rights.

63 Mass. *Records*, IV-I, 29-30.

64 Mass. *Records*, IV-I, 48, 72.

Holyoke and Henry Smith.[65] He then retired to England, a man in his sixties, to live there the rest of his life.

Pynchon's successors carried on his activities with little change. Henry Smith succeeded him in the magistracy.[66] Holyoke and John Pynchon were appointed to administer the freeman's oath in Springfield.[67] The two latter both served on committees to lay out Northampton and Hadley.[68] Pynchon continued and expanded the business, using the overland route to drive cattle to Boston[69] and joining in 1659 in an unfulfilled plan to plant an outpost near the Dutch at Fort Orange.[70] The business history of this group continues after 1660.

The Pynchon enterprises grew up with the growth of western Massachusetts. Political leadership and commercial initiative both developed within the family group. The town of Springfield and the business were founded simultaneously; Northampton, Westfield and Hadley were settled partly at least through the firm's guidance and depended on it for commercial services. On this sector of the Puritan frontier the fur trader, evolving into a promoter and politician, emerged as an important agent of development.

65 Morison, *op. cit.*, pp. 53-54.

66 Mass. *Records*, IV-I, 48.

67 Mass. *Records*, IV-I, 135.

68 Mass. *Records*, IV-I, 136, 368.

69 Judd, *Hadley*, p. 376.

70 Fort Orange became Albany. Mass. *Records*, IV-I, 374.

CHAPTER VIII

THE NEW ENGLAND FRONTIER

MANY towns founded before 1660 do not fall neatly into any one of our categories. They were not the work of a popular minister or a versatile individual entrepreneur. Nor were they the result of a religious schism or the overgrowth of a particular town. The opportunity was there for any handful of families who wanted to petition for a grant, clear land, build houses and engage an unattached graduate of Cambridge or Harvard to preach. From an early date new towns were planted by groups of people for whom such an act was no more than a simple, straightforward and familiar attack on the problem of getting a livelihood.

With the various contingents of the Newtown migration in 1635 and 1636 a group from Dorchester went to settle Windsor and a party from Watertown planted Wethersfield. Dorchester was a town settled by a group from the west of England which had been well-organized before coming to America and were relative strangers to the predominantly East Anglian settlers of the other towns. About 56 or 57 of the 170 men recorded as inhabitants before the end of 1635 transferred their holdings to newcomers and moved to Windsor.[1] Roger Ludlow, who went to Windsor, and Israel Stoughton, who stayed in Dorchester, were involved in political disputes which may have had a bearing on the decision to move,[2] but there is no evidence of strong or general differences of opinion between the removers and those who stayed. The town records show no sign that the emigrants had any difficulty in disposing of their property, and we are left to surmise that willing buyers in Dorchester and vacant lands in Windsor explain their decision.

[1] *History of Dorchester*, pp. 38-99. Only 40 continued as residents of Dorchester, and 6 died before or soon after 1636. 33 are reported to have moved to places other than Windsor and of the remainder no records are found after 1636.

[2] *Op. cit.*, p. 26; Winthrop *Journal*, I, 147, 149.

Much the same explanation may apply to the 41 or so Wethersfield settlers who came from Watertown. The latter was the home of John Oldham who had traded arid explored along the Connecticut coast line and river before it was settled. The town's population was quite possibly growing enough to use up the local supply of land faster than its inhabitants liked, for a little more than a year after the departure of the Wethersfield settlers, " a great part of the chiefe inhabitants " were complaining of " their straitnes of accomodation, & want of medowe " and successfully petitioning for land to start the new town of Sudbury.[3]

Meanwhile the land near the Bay was being explored and disposed of as town grants. Three sites beyond existing towns were noted by the General Court in 1635 as being available, three more in 1636 and more from time to time later.[4] These and other areas became towns after brief and variable periods, Concord having been settled almost immediately and Billerica [5] only after some years. For example Nathaniel Ward, minister at Ipswich, was looking in 1639 for a place where he, his son John, and his son-in-law Giles Firmin might settle together.[6]

3 Mass. *Records*, I, 206, 211.

4 The Court's action consisted of one or more of the following : A statement that the place is to be a plantation, appointment of a surveying party or a committee to license settlers, conditional grant to a group of settlers. Mass. *Records*, I, 141. (Cochichowick or Andover), p. 146 (Wessacution or Newbury), pp. 156-157 (Musketequid or Concord), p. 167 (Wenicunnett or Hampton and Shawshin or Billerica), p. 256 (Cape Ann or Gloucester), p. 271 (Colchester or Salisbury), p. 326 (Nantasket or Hull), etc.

5 *Vide supra*, pp. 66-71.

6 Firmin in a letter (26 Dec. 1639) writes to Governor Winthrop: " My father in law Ward, since his sonne came over, is varey desirous that wee might sett down together, and so that he might leave us together if God should remove him from hence, Because that it cannot be accomplished in this town, is verey desirous to get mee to remove with him to a new plantation. After much perswasion used, consideringe my want of accomodation here (the ground the town having given mee lying 5 miles from me or more) and that the gaines of physick will not find mee with bread, but besides, apprehendinge that it might bee a way to free him from some temptations, and make him more cheerefull and serviceable to the country

The next May the General Court authorized three officials to grant the group Pentucket or Cochicowick [7] and that spring twelve men from Ipswich and Newbury associated with Ward and Firmin, settled at Pentucket.[8] John Ward joined them, in what by then had become the town of Haverhill, about 1643.[9] Nathaniel Ward in that year planned to lay out a colony land grant near the new town,[10] but he and Firmin both returned to England during the 1640's. Newbury, Hampton, Salisbury and Andover formed with Haverhill a chain of towns along the lower Merrimac Valley, planted between 1635 and 1646.

In central Massachusetts a similar series commenced with the planting of Concord in 1635 and Dedham the following year. In addition to the plantations made by older towns Groton (ca 1656), Lancaster and Marlboro (ca 1660) received companies, and the Ipswich group which about 1660 planted Brookfield, a half-way post on the Pynchons' Bay Path, built the outermost and most venturesome of this series. Lancaster was planted on a site called Nashaway, and from the first settlement to the date of full recognition as a town was a longer interval and a more irregular and interrupted growth than in most other towns.

The first party to take an interest in the plantation at Nashaway consisted of a merchant named Thomas King, a minister,

---

or church, have yielded to him. Herein, as I desire your counsel, so I humbly request your favour, that you would be pleased to give us the libertye of choosing a plantation, wee thinke it will be at Pentuckett, or Quichich-chek, by Shawshin: So soon as the season will give us leave to goe, wee shall informe your worship which wee desire: And if that, by the court of election, we cannot gather a company to beegine it, wee will let it fall... If your worship have heard any relation of the places, we should remaine thankful to you, if you would be pleased to counsel us to any of them... wee humbly entreate your secrecy in our desires." Printed in *The Hutchinson Papers*, p. 122; Chase, *History of Haverhill*, pp. 35-36; *Winthrop papers*, IV, 163-164.

7 Mass. *Records*, I, 290.

8 Chase, *History of Haverhill*, p. 38.

9 Chase, *History of Haverhill*, p. 39.

10 Mass. *Records*, II, 38.

Nathaniel Norcross and several other men of Watertown and elsewhere. They made an Indian purchase in 1643, and received a colony grant of a plantation in 1644 and 1645.[11] But this first attempt was apparently an almost complete failure, and in 1647 the undertakers informed the General Court of their desire to withdraw altogether. The Court replied that it "doth not thinke fit to destroy ye said plantation, but rathr to incurage it; onely, in regard ye psons now upon it are so few & unmeete for such a worke, care to be taken to pcure othrs, & in ye meane time to remaine in ye Corts powr to dispose of ye planting & ordring of it." [12] Thus the previous grants were swept away, but the few planters on the spot were given another chance. One of the latter, John Prescott, was ordered in 1650 to "make it sufficjently appeare that Nashaway is a fitt place for a plantacon, so as a ministry may be erected and maintajned there, otherwise the parties there inhabiting shallbe called there hence, and suffered to live wthout the meanes any longer." [13] In 1653 the Court found that there were nine families there, and ordered that the settlement might become a town, provided that all existing settlers and others who had "expended either charge or labor for the benefitt of the place" should be equitably treated in allotments of land even though their rights under earlier grants had been made void under the 1647 order.[14] Lancaster acquired a minister, Joseph Rowlandson, in 1657,[15] and maintained itself as a town although with some

11 Mass. *Records*, II, 75, 136.

12 Mass. *Records*, II, 212. Winthrop ascribes their failure to their inability to gather a proper church, and further recounts that "the persons interested in this plantation, being most of them poor men, and some of them corrupt in judgment, and others profane, it went on very slowly, so as that in two years they had not three houses built there, and he whom they called to be their minister left them for their pains." *Journal*, II, 164-165.

13 Mass. *Records*, IV-I, 22.

14 Mass. *Records*, IV-I, 139-140.

15 Marvin, *History of Lancaster*, p. 98.

difficulties in its local affairs,[16] until it was wiped out temporarily in King Philip's War in 1675.

In Plymouth colony Duxbury was growing as an offshoot of Plymouth by 1636 and was a town of itself by 1640. The old colony's overflow planted Scituate, Marshfield and Bridgewater, while emigrants from Massachusetts settled in Taunton (1638) and Rehoboth (1641) and in the Cape Cod towns of Sandwich and Yarmouth (1638), Barnstable (1639) and Eastham (1651). Connecticut's river towns produced inland offshoots at Farmington (1644) and Simsbury (1648) and that colony received the adherence of Southampton (1644) and Easthampton (1649) on Long Island, where settlers from Massachusetts had planted. Fairfield and Stratford (ca. 1639), Norwalk (1649), Middletown (1651), Stonington (1657) and Norwich (1660) were other Connecticut towns.

Frontier development and town-planting continued beyond 1660, beyond 1776 and as long as there was a frontier to develop. We may wonder even today whether the world has seen the last of Puritanism. Yet the generation of English Puritans who invented a social order and in the process found themselves having to improvise a technique of colonization had a unique historical experience. By 1660 the planting of new towns had become an accustomed and routine part of colonial life. The process still, no doubt, appealed to the emotions as an opportunity for a sort of rebirth and still gave promise of solid material advantages. But the work could go on along well-tried paths and the dangers were understood and could be foreseen.

The New England town originated as an organization to cope with the temporal problems of a Puritan church congregation on the frontier. Town-planting in later times came to serve as a technique of development for groups of frontiersmen to whom religion was a matter of course rather than a dominant motive for withdrawal. Companies of speculators and absentee owners took up grants of town units, drew lots and laid

16 Mass. *Records*, IV-I, 189, 296; IV-II, 556-557. See also Marvin, *History of Lancaster* and Safford, *The Story of Colonial Lancaster*.

out divisions in much the old manner. And the Federal land surveys of the Middle West preserved a vestige of the habit of regarding the township as a normal unit of frontier land development.

An early modification of the pattern, as the transition from the Puritan to the general American frontier came, was the wane of the nucleated form of town plan. In the later seventeenth century the towns on the east bank of the Connecticut river were laying each man's land out as a single long strip extending inland from a relatively narrow river frontage, and so building houses in a long continous row rather than a compact group. The later homestead was more and more likely to be a farmhouse standing on its own tract of land rather than a scattered combination of shares in the town's houselots, field, meadow and upland.[17] In some periods and places, of course, the threat of Indian warfare kept frontier houses huddled close together.

The town-planting movement reached a peak in New England in the 1630's. The rate of increase receded thereafter and the 1650's produced on the average only about one new town a year. After 1660 natural increase and New England's share in the growth of the colonies in general brought about a new cycle of expansion. By that time Puritanism was a vested interest on the defensive. The clear outlines of the compact experimental model of the new order were beginning to blur in the melting pot. The survival of heretical Rhode Island and the flourishing of non-Puritan neighbors in nearby New York and Maine undermined the sense of security through isolation that prevailed in the Puritan colonies when between Canada and Virginia they appeared to be outgrowing all rivals. The Restoration government was a three-pronged attack: it was un-Puritan; it demanded some small measure of religious toleration

17 Akagi, *Town Proprietors in New England*, traces the evolution of towns as units of land ownership through the colonial period. Woodard, *Town Proprietors of Vermont*, describes a late group of towns in which little remains of the institution save an intermediate step in the transfer of land from public to individual ownership.

and (unlike its immediate predecessors) it sent its officers to the colonies backed with authority to enforce its will. The first generation of colonists, English in birth, education and in the social institutions they brought to and built in their colonies, had a free hand to build a new state. Their heirs after 1660 found themselves a part of the British Empire.

The Puritan plan to build a recognizably civilized community of a new and improved design was on the whole a success. The household, the plantation, the church and the adventurer were patterns of behavior adapted from English life and well-suited, as the New England colonists developed them, to frontier conditions. The habit of absorbing population increases by multiplication or division of towns minimized the complexity of administrative units and market contacts for ordinary people, since the colonies could grow fast while each individual town (except the newest) enjoyed relative stability. Some measure of thoughtful planning of town life occurred, and some attempt was made to develop land, timber and water resources in an efficient and unwasteful way.

The Puritans' great failure was in their attempt to maintain social unity through religious orthodoxy. At the beginning they did not doubt that they had the means of discovering the truth, and the power and the duty to suppress deviations from it. But their philosophical method itself tended toward diversity and intellectual individualism, and the conditions of frontier life gave the individualists the means of survival.

BIBLIOGRAPHY

The following list is intended to include all the works mentioned or quoted in the text which follows, and also those works from which I have derived information or ideas which have been valuable or pertinent, but which have not been directly mentioned in the following pages.

The list is classified under five headings:

     I. Colony records
    II. Town records and histories
   III. General history
   IV. Town government and land policy
    V. Puritanism

I. COLONY RECORDS

Connecticut:

    The public records of the colony of Connecticut, prior to the union with the New Haven colony, May, 1665 (Hartford, 1850).

    Records of the Particular Court of Connecticut 1639-1663, Collections of the Connecticut Historical Society (Hartford, 1928).

Massachusetts:

    Records of the governor and company of the Massachusetts Bay in New England, I, II, III, IV (part I) (Boston, 1853-1854).

New Haven:

    Records of the colony and plantation of New Haven, from 1638 to 1649 (Hartford, 1857).

    Records of the colony or jurisdiction of New Haven, from May 1653 to the Union (Hartford, 1858).

Plymouth:

    Records of the colony of New Plymouth in New England, I-IV (Boston, 1855).

    Acts of the commissioners of the United Colonies of New England, in *Records of the colony of New Plymouth in New England*, IX-X (Boston, 1859).

Rhode Island:

    Rhode Island colonial records, I (Providence, 1856).

II. TOWN RECORDS AND HISTORIES

Billerica:

    John Farmer, *Historical memoir of Billerica* (Amherst, Mass., 1816).

    Henry A. Hazen, *History of Billerica, Mass.* (Boston, 1883).

Booton:

  Boston town records 1634-1660, Second report of the record commissioners (Boston, 1877).

Braintree:

  William S. Pattee, *History of Braintree and Quincy* (Quincy, Mass., 1878).
  Records of the town of Braintree 1640-1793 (Randolph, Mass., 1886).

Cambridge:

  Lucius R. Paige, *History of Cambridge 1630-1877* (Boston, 1877).
  The Proprietors' records (Cambridge, Mass., 1896).
  The records of the town of Cambridge (Cambridge, Mass., 1901).

Dorchester:

  Dorchester town records, fourth report of the record commissioners (Boston, 1880).
  The history of the town of Dorchester by a committee of the Dorchester Antiquarian and Historical Society (Boston, 1859).

Exeter:

  Charles H. Bell, *History of the town of Exeter, N. H.* (Exeter, N. H., 1888).
  Exeter plantation covenant, Collections of the New Hampshire Historical Society, I, 147-149.

Hadley:

  Sylvester Judd, *History of Hadley* (Northampton, Mass., 1863).

Haverhill:

  George W. Chase, *History of Haverhill, Massachusetts* (Haverhill, Mass., 1861).

Ipswich:

  Joseph B. Felt, *History of Ipswich, Essex and Hamilton* (Cambridge, Mass., 1834).
  "Ipswich land grants" Essex county historical and genealogical register, I, 163-164, 184-185; II, 10-12, 37-39, 59.
  Thomas F. Waters, *Ipswich in the Massachusetts Bay Colony* (Ipswich, 1905).

Lancaster:

  Abijah P. Marvin, *History of Lancaster, Massachusetts* (Lancaster, Mass., 1879).
  Marion F. Safford, *The story of colonial Lancaster* (Rutland, Vt., 1937).

Lynn:

  Alonzo Lewis and James R. Newhall, *History of Lynn 1629-1864* (Lynn, 1890).

New Haven:

New Haven town records (New Haven, 1917-1919).

New London:

Frances M. Caulkins, *History of New London, Connecticut* (Hartford, 1852).

Newton:

Samuel F. Smith, *History of Newton, Massachusetts* (Boston, 1880).

Northampton:

James R. Trumbull, *History of Northampton* (Northampton, Mass., 1898-1902).

Norwich:

Frances M. Caulkins, *History of Norwich, Connecticut* (Hartford, 1866).

Portsmouth, R. I.:

The early records of the town of Portsmouth (Providence, R. I., 1901).

Rehoboth:

Richard L. Brown, *Early Rehoboth* (Rehoboth, Mass., 1945).

Rowley:

Thomas Gage, *The history of Rowley ... from the year 1639 to the present time* (Boston, 1840).

Roxbury:

Roxbury land and church records, sixth report of the record commissioners (Boston, 1880).

Charles McEllis, *History of Roxbury, Mass.* (Boston, 1847).

Springfield:

Simeon E. Baldwin, " The secession of Springfield from Connecticut." Publications of the Colonial Society of Massachusetts, XII, 55.

Henry M. Burt, *The first century of the history of Springfield. The official records from 1636 to 1736* (Springfield, Mass., 1898).

Mason A. Green, *Springfield, 1636-1886* (Springfield, Mass., 1888).

Warwick:

Oliver P. Fuller, *The history of Warwick, Rhode Island* (Providence, 1875).

Watertown:

Henry Bond, *Genealogies of the families and descendants of the early settlers of Watertown, ... to which is appended the early history of the town* (Boston, 1860).

Watertown records (Watertown, Mass., 1894).

114

BIBLIOGRAPHY

Wethersfield:

Sherman W. Adams, *Ancient Wethersfield* (New York, 1904).

Windsor:

Some early records and documents of and relating to the town of Windsor, Connecticut 1639-1681 (Hartford, 1930).

Henry R. Stiles, *Ancient Windsor* (New York, 1859).

III. GENERAL HISTORY

James T. Adams, *The founding of New England* (Boston, 1921).

Charles M. Andrews, *The colonial period of American history* (New Haven, 1934-1937).

Edward E. Atwater, *History of the colony of New Haven* (New Haven, 1881).

William Bradford, *History of Plymouth plantation*. Original narratives of early American history (New York, 1908).

Charles E. Banks, *The planters of the Commonwealth 1620-1640* (Boston, 1930).

Isabel M. Calder, *The New Haven colony* (New Haven, 1934).

A century of population growth, U. S. Department of Commerce and Labor, Bureau of the Census, S. N. D. North, director (Washington, 1909).

Franklin B. Dexter, "Estimates of population in the American colonies," report of the Council of the American Antiquarian Society (Worcester, Mass., 1887).

John Fiske, *The beginnings of New England* (Boston, 1889).

Charles A. Flagg, *A guide to Massachusetts local history* (Salem, 1907).

Samuel R. Gardner, *History of England from the accession of James I to the outbreak of the civil war* (London, 1883-1884).

Evarts B. Greene and Virginia Harrington, *American population before the census of 1790* (New York, 1932).

George H. Haynes, "The tale of the Tantiusques, an early mining venture in Massachusetts," *Proceedings* of the American Antiquarian Society, 2d series, XIV, 471-497.

William Hubbard, *History of New England* (Reprinted in Massachusetts Historical Society Collections, series 2, V, VI).

Edward Johnson, *The wonder working providence of Zion's saviour in New England,* Original narratives of early American history (New York, 1910).

The Hutchinson papers, publications of the Prince society, II (Albany, 1865).

Cotton Mather, *Magnalia Christi Americana,* 1st American ed., from the London edition of 1702.

Lois K. Mathews, *The expansion of New England* (Boston, 1909).

Lawrence S. Mayo, *The Winthrop family in America* (Boston, 1948).

Samuel E. Morison, *Builders of the Bay colony* (Boston, 1930).

——, *The founding of Harvard College* (Cambridge, Mass., 1935).

——, "William Pynchon, the founder of Springfield," *Proceedings* of the Massachusetts Historical Society, LXIV, 67.

Arthur P. Newton, *The colonising activities of the English Puritans* (New Haven, 1914).

Herbert L. Osgood, *The American colonies in the seventeenth century* (New York, 1904-1907).

New Englands first fruits (London, 1643) reprinted in Massachusetts Historical Society collections, series 1, I, 242.

Benjamin Trumbull, *A complete history of Connecticut* (New Haven, 1818).

Thomas F. Waters, *A sketch of the life of John Winthrop the younger, founder of Ipswich, Massachusetts* (Ipswich, 1899).

William B. Weeden, *Economic and social history of New England* (Boston, 1890).

Frederick L. Weis, *The colonial churches and the colonial clergy of New England* (Lancaster, Mass., 1936).

Thomas J. Wertenbaker, *The Puritan Oligarchy* (New York, 1947).

John Winthrop, *Journal*, "History of New England" 1630-1649, Original narratives of early American history (New York, 1908).

Winthrop papers, III, IV, V (Boston, 1943, 1944, 1947).

Robert C. Winthrop, *Life and letters of John Winthrop* (Boston, 1864-1867).

William Wood, *New Englands prospect* (London, 1634) reprinted in Publications of the Prince Society, I.

Wyllys papers, Collections of the Connecticut Historical Society, XXVII.

IV. Town Government and Land Policy

Herbert B. Adams, *The germanic origin of New England towns*, Johns Hopkins University studies in historical and political science, first series no. 2 (Baltimore, 1883).

Roy H. Akagi, *The town proprietors of the New England colonies* (Philadelphia, 1924).

Charles M. Andrews, *River towns of Connecticut*, Johns Hopkins University studies in historical and political science, VII (Baltimore, 1889).

Melville Eggleston, *The land system of the New England colonies*, Johns Hopkins University studies in historical and political science, fourth series nos. 11, 12 (Baltimore, 1886).

Howard L. Gray, *English field systems* (Cambridge, Mass., 1915).

Anne B. MacClear, *Early New England towns* (New York, 1908).

John Pratt, "Apology of writing to England," Records of the Massachusetts Bay Colony, I, 358 (undated but probably about 1635).

John F. Sly, *Town government in Massachusetts (1620-1930)* (Cambridge, Mass., 1930).

"Maintenance of ministers in the county of Suffolk," Massachusetts Historical Society collections, series 3, I, 49.

Paul Vinogradoff, *The growth of the manor* (London, 1905).

Florence Woodard, *Town proprietors of Vermont* (New York, 1936).

V. Puritanism

Charles F. Adams, *Three episodes in Massachusetts history* (Boston, 1892).
Perry Miller, *The New England Mind* (New York, 1939).
——, *Orthodoxy in Massachusetts* (Cambridge, Mass., 1933).
—— and T. H. Johnson (editor), *The Puritans* (New York, 1938).

INDEX

Pawtuxit, 46
Penobscot, 51
Pequot, 34, 35, 50, 97, 98, 100
Peters, Thomas, 98
Piscataqua, 94
Plantation, 17, 18, 19, 108
Plymouth, 13, 20, 24, 31, 33, 36, 45,
  48, 51, 71, 74, 88, 108
Poor, 19, 20, 21, 38
Population, 15, 16, 28, 29, 43, 50, 52,
  105, 110
Portsmouth, R. I., 47, 53, 76, 79, 80
Prescott, John, 107
Providence, 18, 38, 41, 45. 46, 53, 56,
  76, 79, 80
Prudden, Peter, 89
Pynchon, John, 55, 102, 103, 106
Pynchon, William, 50, 55, 99, 100,
  101, 102, 103

Quaker, 80
Quinnipiack, *see* New Haven

Rate, 37, 41, 57, 64, 69, 70
Reading, 71
Rehoboth, 108
Rhode Island, 31, 33, 38, 41, 47, 48,
  63, 76, 79, 80, 98, 109
Rogers, Ezekiel, 44, 54, 90, 91
Rowlandson, Joseph, 107
Rowley, 44, 54, 90, 91, 96
Roxbury, 49, 50, 67, 82, 87, 99, 100
Russell, John, 83, 84, 85

Salem, 16, 44, 45, 71, 74, 75, 79, 96
Salisbury, 31, 44, 106
Saltonstall Park, 35
Saltworks, 34, 96
Salvation, 40, 41, 47, 76, 77
Sandwich, 51, 108
Say and Seal, Lord, 95
Saybrook, 36, 93, 96, 98, 101
Scituate, 51, 108
Seditious libel, 78
Selectmen, 22
Servant, 20, 21, 38
Shawshin, *see* Billerica
Shepard, Thomas, 66
Ship-building, 29, 55
Simsbury, 71, 108
Smith, Henry (minister at Wethers-
  field), 83
Smith, Henry (of Springfield), 103

Southampton, 108
Southold, 89, 91
Springfield, 50, 71, 82, 84, 98, 100,
  101, 102, 103
Stamford, 83, 90
Stone, Samuel, 66, 83, 84
Stonington, 108
Stoughton, Israel, 104
Stratford, 108
Sudbury, 44, 71, 105
Surveys, 31, 32, 44, 66
Symonds, Samuel, 95

Taunton, 51, 108
Thompson, *see* Tompson
Timber, 25, 27, 29, 34, 52
Toleration, 46, 48
Tompson, William, 64
Topsfield, 75

United Colonies, 90, 98, 102

Vane, Henry, 77, 78
Village, 44, 52, 53, 61, 66, 67, 69, 71,
  72, 73, 75

Ward, John, 91, 105, 106
Ward, Nathaniel, 91, 95, 105, 106
Warehouse Point, 102
Warham, John, 83, 84, 85
Warwick, 41, 48, 53, 77
Watertown, 44, 49, 69, 70, 71, 82,
  101, 105, 107
Wells, 48
Wenham, 74
Westfield, 71, 103
Wethersfield, 50, 82, 83, 84, 85, 89,
  104, 105
Weymouth, 43, 51
Wheelwright, John, 47, 48, 63, 64,
  77, 78, 79, 81
Whitfield, Henry, 90
Whiting, Samuel, 70
Williams, Roger, 17, 31, 45, 46, 48,
  76, 79, 80
Windsor, 35, 50, 71, 82, 83, 84, 85,
  104
Winthrop, John, 34, 35, 49, 56, 61,
  62, 94
Winthrop, John, Jr., 34, 55, 91-99
Woburn, 68, 70-71

Yarmouth, 51, 91, 108
Younge, John, 89